T0003811

In loving memory of my father, Peter, whose last words
to me were: 'It's okay to make a little green.'

Remington Donovan

Prosperity Practices

Harnessing the power of positive thinking to get the life you want

Hardie Grant

BOOKS

What is prosperity?

Prosperity is different for everybody. It could be money, time, love, health... the possibilities are endless.

Some people want more time to enjoy their life. Some people want more money. Some people want more time *and* more money. Some people want more love. Prosperity for one person might be a beautiful studio apartment in the city of their dreams. For someone else, it might be a mansion in the countryside, a sailing boat, being able to go on mountain hikes or spending time with family and friends. My intention with this book is to share techniques and practices to help you reach your goals, whatever they may be.

Prosperity, on some level, is a mindset. It's not limited to the things that we have or our material possessions (although these are an important part of prosperity). It relates to the whole of our lives, to our whole spiritual being.

My personal prosperity journey is one of transformation, from despair and depravity, barely surviving, to living generously. I was so poor that I literally had to scrape together change from the deep recesses of my couch just to take a bus, hoping that when I got to my destination I would be able to get a ride home after the event. I know what it's like to be flat broke and depressed. I felt like I'd never meet anybody, that I'd always be single and didn't deserve the kind of love I longed for. I freakin' get it.

Out of those gnarly negative experiences, I've created a wonderful life. I managed to transform all that desperation into a very successful six-figure income that is growing every year. I married my soulmate and life partner. We have a beautiful baby boy. I've created a living and a business based on the things that I love the most. I've been able to turn my work, which is who I am, into an entirely self-supporting operation. I work for myself. I work with my partner. We live in a crazy-cool house I seriously never imagined being able to call home. We even own a real full-size caboose. I have a car, for which I'm very grateful. I have learned the value of money. I have learned the value of time. I have learned the value of gratitude and I have definitely learned the value of love. I feel I have more love, money and time than I ever imagined was possible. Yet I'm still growing, improving and harnessing more prosperity.

There is no quick fix. There is no cure-all. Everything I'm sharing in this book is what I have applied to my own life that has absolutely worked for me, and I have seen work for others.

My personal story started with needing more love and acceptance. I had to work on creating prosperity daily. The emotional, internal shift eventually led to financial upgrades, which led to greater opportunities. Prosperity adds more prosperity. I cherish now having time to enjoy my life.

When calling in prosperity, I encourage you to look at all the different parts of your life. What are your career goals? What do you seek professionally? Do you need more time? Or love? Or money? Don't compare yourself to other people; just focus on what would make a difference to you now. Where would you like to grow, and what does the life that you want look and feel like? This is personal to you. What do you love to do? Can you imagine yourself making money doing that?

While reading and applying these practices to your life, be open to something bigger and better than you have been imagining. Trust the miracles that come your way. Embrace the beautiful, and sometimes scary, moments of transformation. When you are open to prosperity, you become more prosperous. You were already born a success. It's time to reclaim it.

How this book came to be

Years ago, I found myself at a very low point in my life.

I had lost my job, and this triggered a whole series of events that led to a severe suicidal depression. I had been in the same type of job, working in restaurants, for many years, and I felt like I had lost everything. I had no hope. I'd just moved to Los Angeles and I was in a new city that was huge and overwhelming. I had no place to go back to. I didn't really have anywhere to go. I'd never felt so alone in my life.

I know what it's like to lose everything. I know what it's like to feel like the only solution is not to be here any more. I know what it's like to feel like there's no way out. I know what it's like to feel like nothing is ever going to work out, that nothing will line up, that peace and serenity will always be strangers, that meeting someone is impossible, that being broke and alone is inevitable.

It felt like I was born in the wrong time.

I was always a day late and a dollar short. After years of living this way, I hit rock bottom.

I wanted to die. I apologise if that's triggering, but that's my story and that's how bad it got for me.

I'd moved to Los Angeles in hope of expanding my comedy career. I had a potential television show in the works. I thought I'd be a TV writer. I was really attached to that dream for some time. Then things changed, and I hit that rock bottom. I'd moved to the iconic Venice Beach neighbourhood of LA with a suitcase full of dreams and a carry-on full of hope, only to find myself soon writing a suicide note. As I was writing my farewell, my pen completely ran out of ink.

This was a brand-new pen that I'd literally just taken out of the package. At this time in my life, I was performing a lot. I was writing a lot of comedy with a pad and pen. I felt like such a pathetic loser at life that I couldn't even write a suicide note. I was such a failure that I couldn't even buy a pen that actually worked.

And that's what so much of my life felt like then: complete failure. Like many of us, I had always felt like I had potential, that I could go on to do great things. But my life was a daily struggle to carve out a small existence renting a bedroom. I'd been working in the same kind of restaurant job that I had done for the last 20-something years of my life. It wasn't even anything high dollar or rewarding, and certainly wasn't fulfilling any more. I was a life misfit. But my pen running out of ink was a big turning point for me.

In that moment, something bigger than me, some higher energy, force, power or love – or maybe simply the auspicious line-up of coincidences that meant I got a pen that didn't work – was enough to interrupt the downward spiral to which I had become very committed. That pen actually saved my life. It forced me to make a decision that was for me. I needed to change my life, which meant changing myself.

That's where my prosperity journey began. I want you to know that no matter which path you're coming from, these practices will meet you there.

Please, if you are someone who struggles, don't give up. There is a way through every block.

It took me a few years to climb out of that hole. I had to let go. I had to let go of forcing a specific job or a specific career. Inevitably, as promised, a lot of other opportunities opened up. Maybe I'm not writing for television, but I write books on prosperity. I wrote a book on numerology. I'm currently working on other books. I get to share and teach, and I get to do what I most sincerely love. I love creating stories. I love communicating and writing. So maybe it's not TV deals, but it is book deals. And so, I let go, and I got better at showing up.

Why this book?

The idea for this book came about because of something I call the 'Prosperity Family'.

A few years ago, my wife and I decided to get a group of people together, a little collective, for a 40-day commitment to a particular prosperity exercise. The collective increased their prosperity in all things, from relationships and bank accounts to joy and freedom.

This book is a compilation of the tried-and-true practices we did as part of this collective, and the many other practices I utilise regularly. There isn't a practice in here that I have not done myself.

The intent of this book is to share a variety of practices that you can do as casually or as intensely as you like.

In a deep meditation, it came to me to create something that is the culmination of all these practices. Something pragmatic and approachable to help people get a little more in tune with their infinite self, and create more optimism, wellbeing and a nicer life.

Welcome to the Prosperity Family.

How to use this book

This book is a culmination of practices I have learned throughout my life. Some are from spiritual teachers and traditions. Some are from life coaches and other people in the field of transformative arts. Others are just little gems I've picked up along the way. Every practice in this book is something I have personally done and have had success with. I suppose it's a 'greatest hits' of techniques that have served me and others well. They vary in their roots and ideology. The common theme is self-improvement, with a focus on having a more prosperous and abundant life, whatever that means for you and your desires. Abundance starts within. It's always an inside job. These practices have proven themselves successful for so many. They work if you work them. Some may resonate more than others for you. You are welcome to do as many or as few as you like. There is no specific order. Some of these may have a greater effect on you than others. Some will lead to 'aha' moments that change everything. Some may

Start shifting your attitude & energy towards what you have and the blessings in your life.

Start to shift your attitude and energy towards what you have and the blessings in your life. Whatever you focus your energy on is going to create more of whatever that is. It's all too easy to fall into the trap of thinking about everything you don't have and everything you would like to have.

It is quite easy to spiral into a gridlock of lack and negativity. A 'woe is me' attitude: 'I don't have enough money,' 'I will always be alone,' 'I could have done big things if only... [fill in the blank],' 'I will always be miserable in my job.' The list could go on and on and on. You get the point. It's easy to get absorbed in that stinking thinking.

Gratitude is a powerful tool for shifting out of that mindset. Gratitude helps you see what you have, and an attitude of gratitude can shift your whole vibe, from stress, fear, regret and loss into love, optimism, courage, hope and abundance.

Free-flowing gratitude list

Shifting your perspective immediately alleviates a lot of worry and concern. The idea of the law of attraction, meaning like attracts like, is that it starts with an internal frequency, an internal vibration or an internal headspace, and vibrates out to find a match. Practising gratitude focuses your energy on abundance rather than lack, and that shift of gears and sense of optimism can be very powerful Shifting gears and creating a little bit more optimism can be very powerful.

Practice •

Write an unedited free-flowing list of every single thing you're grateful for. Maybe it's the smell of lavender, a book that you love, or a teacher you had as a kid. It could be as small as your toothbrush or as big as the day your child was born. It doesn't matter. Nobody has to read it. This list will help you refocus on everything you already have. When you see that, attracting the things you want but don't have yet becomes easier.

Remind yourself to move into that gratitude headspace when you find yourself focused only on everything you don't have. This is often referred to as a 'scarcity mindset', which attracts and amplifies situations of lack. Like attracts like.

Fake it till you make it. We don't have to do any of this perfectly.

The first time I did this gratitude practice, I decided to make a list of everything I was grateful for. I was grateful for every personal possession that I had. I was grateful for my shampoo. I was grateful for my down duvet (comforter). I was grateful for my motorcycle boots, even though I didn't have a motorcycle. I was grateful for my parents. I was grateful for my friends. I was grateful for the sunset.

I probably listed a few hundred things. I grabbed a notebook and went for it. My ego thought it was dumb and cheesy, but I let go and got into the flow.

Even when things are going really well, I will still sometimes catch myself moving into a scarcity mindset. As my life expands, so have my concerns. Making a little gratitude list helps me come back to centre. It can be short and sweet or it can be long and everything. I recommend doing both. This practice can be done whenever needed. Allow it to be easy and freeing.

Daily gratitude list

Every single day, just after you wake up and before you go to sleep, write at least three things that you're grateful for. This is a great way to start and end the day. Keep a notebook beside your bed and write your gratitude list as soon as you open your eyes each morning and again before you go to sleep. As a dear friend of mine likes to say, 'Count your blessings instead of sheep.'

Multiply prosperity and do this exercise with a friend (or friends), family or a large group of people. Check in with one another. There's no censoring or judgement; it will get you going to simply share things that you're grateful for.

You could do it as an email chain, text thread, phone call, whatever works for you. Share *three* things you're grateful for every single day.

It's a lot of fun to share with other people. The collective energy creates a sweet, supportive vibe.

It's nice to work together with people who encourage each other's successes and prosperity. Count your blessings, not your stresses.

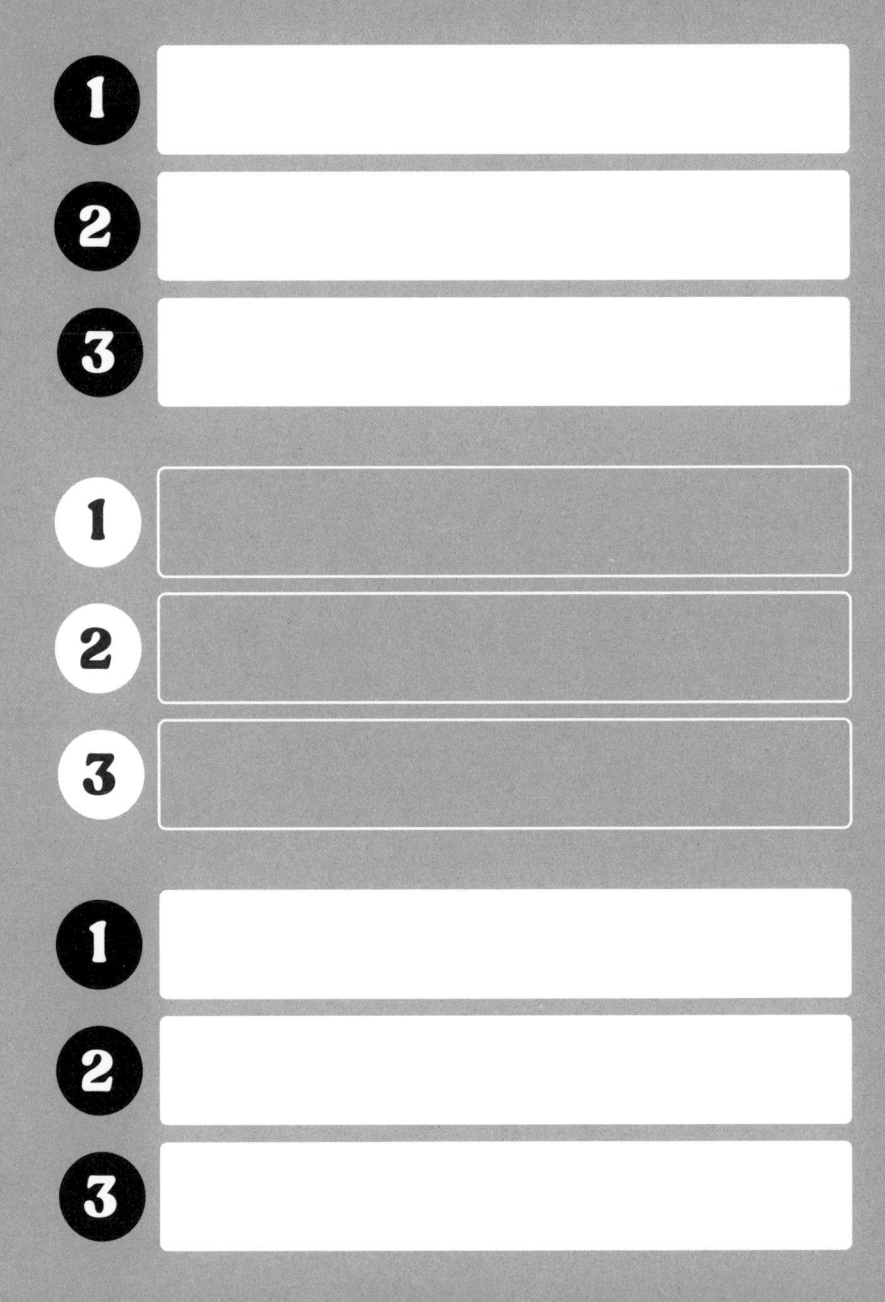

Be here now

Another key concept of gratitude is being here now. This is a spiritual teaching that's rooted in a deeper philosophy of life. Be here now means *everything is okay, and you have every single thing that you need in this moment. Never forget that.*

Practice •

Take a deep breath, live in this moment and realise that, at this very second, you do have exactly what you need. Of course, this doesn't mean you're not aware of the future and things you have to plan and bills you have to pay and appointments and meetings you need to attend, but a lot of opportunities can open up to us if we stay in this space.

You will start to let go of regret from the past, that sense of 'should've, would've, could've'. You will let go of fear, worry and anxiety about the future, all of which trample down on our energy and negatively affect our headspace and psyche, which is exactly how *not* to attract prosperity and emotional wellbeing. These are not ways of attracting opportunity. So, when you stay a little grateful, when you decide, 'Okay, in this moment, I am here, I am present, I really do have everything I need,' channels will open up for you.

You're always in the centre of the universe, and you are a part of something so much bigger than yourself.

It's all right here.
It's all right here.

When I was about eight or nine,
I remember being at an event where
someone read from a collection of
stories written by people in prison.

One of the stories, written by a man
serving a life sentence, finished with,
'It's all right here. It's all right here.' I have
always thought to myself, this person was
in a dire situation but was open enough
to realise that everything he needed was
not only right there, but that it was *all*
right there.

It got me thinking from a young age
that wherever you are, it really is all right
there. That man chose to stay optimistic,
humble and, above all, grateful.

I grew up in a spiritual community, an
ashram and a commune. I was taught
that the universe is infinite. That man's
story always made me think that if the
universe is infinite no matter where you
are, you're always in the centre of the
universe and you are a part of something
so much bigger than yourself. The more
you get centred in that, the more flow of
opportunity there is.

This is a devout meditation and a lifestyle
practice. If someone serving a lifetime
sentence could believe and embody that,
then you can start here, where you're at.

Start where you're at

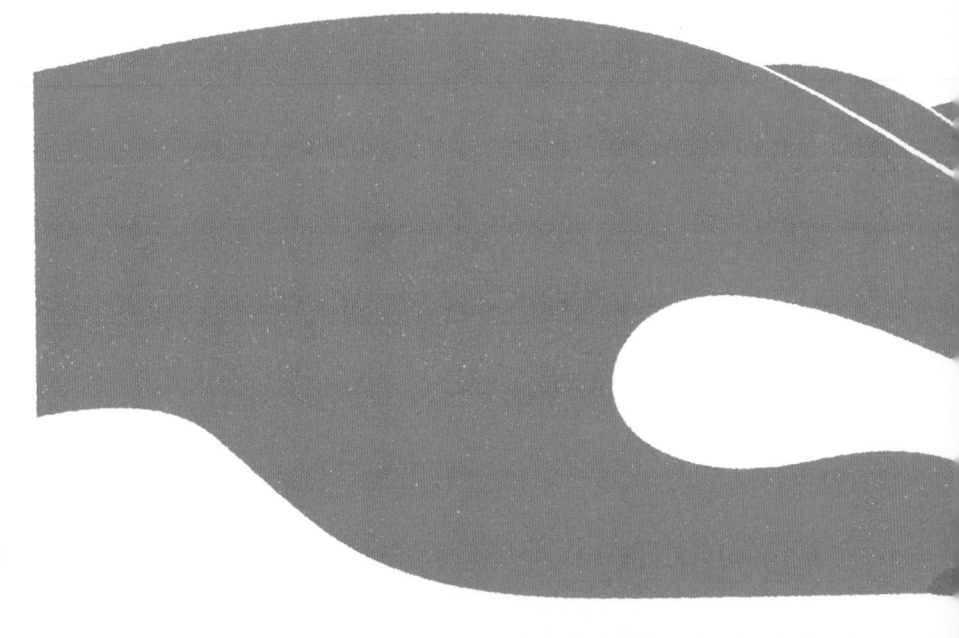

Whatever your goals may be to get ahead in life, start where you are and see where that takes you. As you begin to get the ball rolling, this creates an energy and a shift, after which things start to line up. So wherever you're at, whatever the project, whatever the idea, whatever it is you're trying to manifest, begin to work through the process.

There is a yogic teaching: 'When the time is on you, start and the pressure will be off.'

It's about rolling up your sleeves, doing your due diligence, not getting caught in overthinking, over-strategising or over-planning. Trust me, there's plenty of time for that, but if you just get the notion of being here now and saying, 'OK, let's go!' then doors will open. Your brain will start to process a lot more, in ways you never thought possible.

Just start.

It's never too late

This was huge for me.

I feel like I'm a late bloomer with everything: marriage, family, career. While I was in the process of getting my act together I often fell into the regret of I could've, would've, should've – if only I'd done this when I was younger, if only I'd put more of my attention towards making money or having a career, or being honest about who I was and doing the things that I really loved, well, that would've been great. But that's not how it went. I wasted a lot of time on drugs and booze, squandering my potential (and bank account) and never getting anywhere. Getting into the mindset that it's never too late made such a difference to me.

Practice •

Know that lost dreams do awaken. It is never too late to create success and opportunity. You are never too old. On the other hand, you're never too young. You can do it. You can succeed now. You can succeed – starting here.

I let go of, 'Oh, I'm broke. I'm in my forties and I'm going to need £100,000 to invest in marketing and website design and whatnot.' I didn't have that, but I had passion. I took stock of the things that I love that I was good at. I started where I was, and I started to grow. I felt the universe work with me because I aligned myself with a different mindset, one of opportunity. And I practiced gratitude. I put in the work.

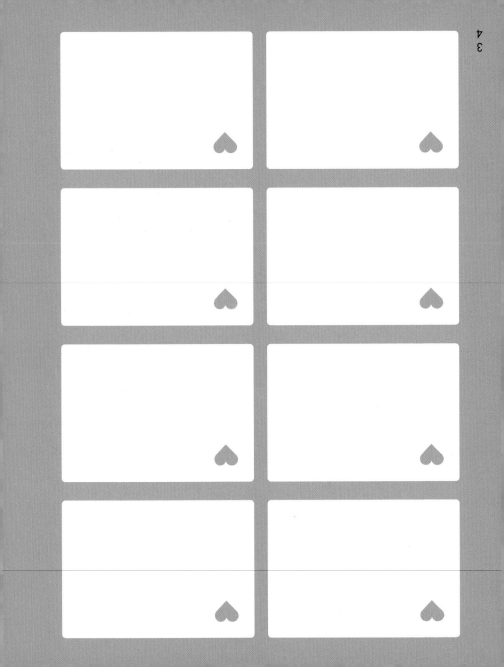

Love list

As The Beatles famously said, 'All you need is love.'

In my line of work, I encounter so many people looking for love. I hear long lists of what they want in a partner or how they wish their partner would change. If they're not looking for romance, they want to be able to *do* what they love. What I rarely hear people saying is what they have to offer in a relationship or in life. I don't think I've had anyone tell me how loving and amazing they would be in a romantic relationship if one did indeed show up, or how lovingly and enthusiastically they would embrace doing the activities they love in life.

Practice •

Make a love list.

Write down everything in the language of love. This is very similar to a gratitude list, but replace the words 'I am grateful for' with 'I love'.

For example:

I love my son.

I love my wife.

I love coffee.

I love my home.

And so on.

This practice is great for getting in touch with the love that's already within. Get used to sharing and offering your love to the world. Like I said: fall in love with the life you have, and you'll have a life you love.

Fear of failure
/ fear of success

I recall an interview with the actor Jim Carrey where he shared a story about his dad. His father was a noted jazz musician who gave up his career to work at an accounting firm. After many years of dedication, his employer let him go. Jim Carrey said that because of this, he learned you can fail at doing something you don't want to do so, you might as well try succeeding at what you'd like to be doing.

I mean... we're all going to die anyway. So why not go for what you want?

Mantra •

Don't let your fear of failure or fear of success (which can be just as scary) get in the way of having a wonderfully fulfilling life.

Take cold showers

A great way to get out of your comfort zone is by taking cold showers. Yes, cold showers. You can go down a deep rabbit hole exploring all the physiological and psychological benefits of this practice but, for the sake of this book, it's about doing something that will feel uncomfortable at first.

Push through the resistance.

Endure the cold.

Get out of your comfort zone. If you keep it up, you will start to love it. Set a timer and do this for 2–3 minutes. See what starts to open up for you.

The comfort zone is where dreams go to die. If it's not cold showers, try something else that challenges your comfort zone. Take an improv or public-speaking class. It's up to you. I took an acting class in Los Angeles from one of those renowned A-list acting coaches. It was terrifying. My ego was put in check every single class. It was one of the most challenging things I've ever done. I'm not an actor, but I learned how to allow a teacher to guide me. I learned how to not take it personally. I respected this teacher very much.

Doing things that push the envelope translates to other areas in your life. You will become more empowered to take a chance on yourself, to take a chance on destiny.

What do I love to do?

Ask yourself what you would love to do for a living or just ask yourself 'What do I love?' and see what comes up.

For this practice, sit in a meditative position. Breathe deeply and consciously. Allow yourself to relax. Now take your left hand and put it in the centre of your chest, which is your heart centre. Place your right hand on top of the left. Continue to breathe deeply, close your eyes and feel that space. Once you've cleared your mind, ask yourself, 'What do I love to do the most?'

Allow an answer. If it feels forced, try again. Breathe. Relax. Let the words or experience come to you. Go with the flow. You will start to see, 'Oh, this is what I love.'

(See page 102 for the 'Three-part 1-minute breath' practice if you need help.)

You have unique gifts, talents and purpose. Your soul has a mission. You were born to fulfil your destiny. When we align ourselves with a higher order and a higher purpose, we turn our chaos into the cosmos. The cosmos is the flow of nature.

If you're lost or don't know what you want, this practice will help you begin to gain a sense of what you do love. The channels that need to open, will.

So, employ this practice from time to time. Check in with yourself. Get a refresh. You may find that what you love doesn't have to be your job. However, as things start to line up, what you love can turn into that.

As I said earlier: fall in love with the life you have, and you'll have a life you love. It is when we're in that headspace that change happens easily. Start flowing and creating assets out of the work you love. When you love something, your life is going to flow a lot better.

Here are some things that have come up for me in the past through this practice: I love teaching and talking to people. I love public speaking. I love being

with my wife and my son. I love signing books. I love talking about this work. I love sharing it. I love meditation. I love the deeper, mystical, emotional side of this work. I love creating community. Essentially this is my life now. I feel very blessed that I get to do it all with my wife and my son.

I started with acceptance. I fell in love with the life I had, which on the outside sucked. I had no money. I was living in somebody's kitchen nook with no privacy. I am grateful to this person, forever, for my whole life. They saved me. It didn't matter that I could barely afford lunch; I was just grateful for a chance to live.

I got in touch with something greater by loving my small world as it was. By accepting it, the things that I really loved started to reveal themselves. They became the things that make up my life as a whole. I don't have a separate job to go to. Everything I do is an extension of myself: the books that I write, the classes I teach, the clients I see, the time I get to spend with my family. I do what I love, and I love what I do.

I assure you, if I can do all of this, so can you.

Self-acceptance

Gratitude is an action. It is a practice and a state of being. Self-acceptance creates gratitude and vice versa.

In order to truly accept yourself, you must let go of perfection. Perfection is a big growth-blocker. It keeps people trapped. It will prevent you from taking chances on yourself. Where gratitude helps you feel good about yourself, perfectionism will always be moving the goal posts, so you're never enough.

Don't let perfection be the enemy of the good.

If you feel good about yourself, you feel safe. You're naturally more self-accepting, and definitely more willing to take a chance on yourself. In other words, you're not feeling so uptight about how perfect everything has to be that you rigidly miss the moment you've been waiting for. So, ease up. Allow compassion. Real compassion is acceptance of others and acceptance of self.

There is a yogic teaching that goes, 'Understand through compassion or you will misunderstand the times.'

This is what I like to call radical self-acceptance. If you just accept exactly where you are, and that you have what you need right here, right now, you can easily step into a state of self-love. As the teaching goes, 'You can love everybody, but you don't have to like everybody.' You can love yourself even if you don't like yourself. Stop creating a show that nobody is watching. Open up and lighten up. This is an opportunity to get free. You will soon love *and* like yourself. Love creates forgiveness, acceptance and more love.

Sometimes it's as simple as saying, 'I feel good about myself. I feel good about my life.' If you have a job that you hate, work out what you're grateful for; you may find yourself in a new position before long.

Worrying is praying for things you don't want.

Worrying is praying for things you
don't want.

By now, you know that if you just keep
adding more stress, more fear, more
worry, more negativity, then guess what?
You become an energetic magnet for
more stress, more fear, more worry, more
negativity. When you're not worried,
you're allowing. When your hands are
open, they're not tight fists holding on
to the little you do have. So, if you have
love and self-acceptance, more love
and more self-acceptance will show up.

Practice •

**Unclench your fists, relax your
jaw, open your hands and
receive. You are creating the
space to receive the blessings.
That is a state of prosperity.**

Self-acceptance is the key to freedom.
There is a teaching that says the universe
is ready to serve you if you just be you.
It sounds like the simplest thing, because
it is, but somehow, along the way, we've
made it one of the hardest.

These practices help you to be you.
The more 'good' you add, the more you
crowd out the 'bad'. Who you are is
happy, who you are is joyous, who
you are is free.

You were born a success

Practice •

This is your mantra:

'Success is inevitable. I agree to be great.
I surrender to the greatness of God.'

Sit in a comfortable position and
meditate on this mantra.

Alternatively, write it on a sticky note
and place it on your bathroom mirror
to read any chance you get, or set it
as a daily reminder on your phone.

Note: When I say 'God', I'm not
assigning any spiritual or religious
tradition to it. The above prayer is an
affirmation that was taught to me. In this
context, consider 'God' the higher order
of something more powerful than you
are; something that is helping you align
with your own greatness, purpose
and destiny.

Assume everyone else is doing their best

This is a wonderful practice for forgiving others and letting them be. You're going to be way less angry, uptight and controlling over how everybody else should be based on your self-imposed will. You're going to just let it slide.

Practice •

Every time someone does something that annoys you or makes you angry, just think, 'Hey, they're doing their best,' and let it go.

This practice creates an opportunity for ease, an opportunity for peace, and an opportunity for greater love, especially in today's world, where people are glued to their social media and everybody has an opinion about everything, everybody's an expert on everything, and everybody feels entitled to judge and criticise others. There are some horrifically sad stories of people being abused or ostracised, losing their jobs and families, or being pushed to the point of suicide. There's tragedy left and right, all because we live in a world where everybody is demanding and critical.

Don't compare

Practice •

**Stop comparing
yourself to others.**

The universe is abundant. There is more
than enough for everyone. If you are
someone who puts themselves out there,
remember that the only people who
criticise are those doing less than you.

It goes both ways.

Do everything with excellence

Show up doing the best you can, with as much excellence as you can, and let go of your preconceived ideas of how it should all be.

When you're uptight and caught up in the end result, you will feel hopelessly crushed if it doesn't play out the way you think it should. If you can enjoy the process, and show up with excellence as your priority, often the results can be far greater than those you anticipated in the first place.

I was taught to do everything with excellence, whatever the task. Even when I was making £9.70 ($11) an hour working in a health-food store as a 40-something-year-old adult, and was feeling down on myself, that I was just a loser of a man, I would still say, 'Okay, I'm going to suit up, I'm going to show up, I'm going to do this job to the best of my ability, I'm going to learn and I'm going to be proficient.' Before long, I became the go-to guy for supplement advice in Los Angeles working at the top health-food store.

Because of that excellence, I was offered a slightly higher-paying job selling vitamins. I didn't see this as my life's work, and I almost didn't take it, but I decided to put my ego aside and go for it. And it was where I met my now wife. She came in looking for immunity supplements while working on a demanding film. Thanks to performing with excellence and choosing to be an expert, I was able to guide her to make great vitamin choices – and, more importantly, husband choices.

As a case study: when I was working in vitamins, I took my time and I learned so much. That job in and of itself went nowhere, but it did open other channels for me.

I met a lot of people that are still my friends, clients and students to this day. I learned an enormous amount about health and nutrition. I met the person I would marry and start a family with.

It was a springboard, and it led me to what I'm doing now, specifically because I stayed open, respectful and present to the possibility by doing everything with excellence.

Excellence leads to accountability. Accountability leads to trust. People trusted me. My deeper work has always been esoteric spirituality. I do believe selling vitamins with excellence opened up opportunities for the work I do today. I use esoteric wisdom, numerology, tarot and astrology to counsel, help and teach people – and this is the work I've loved my whole life. I use these tools and techniques to help others become more prosperous. This is my jam. This is my destiny. Excellence creates destiny.

I agreed to do that job. It was a huge pivotal and transitional point in my life. Showing up and doing things with excellence creates a different frequency. So many of these practices come down to a change in mindset, which changes your own frequency to attract more. If I do things with excellence, I attract more excellent opportunities. There's a level of authenticity and honesty required that never ceases to delight the practitioner, plus everyone you come into contact with. It's contagious.

- **Practise gratitude and love. Loving the life you have will lead you to a life you love.**

  - **Accept who you are and where you are, and start here. It's never too late.**

- **Let go of fear and preconceptions, and step out of your comfort zone.**

  - **Believe that others are doing their best.**

- **Always do everything with excellence.**

Part two:

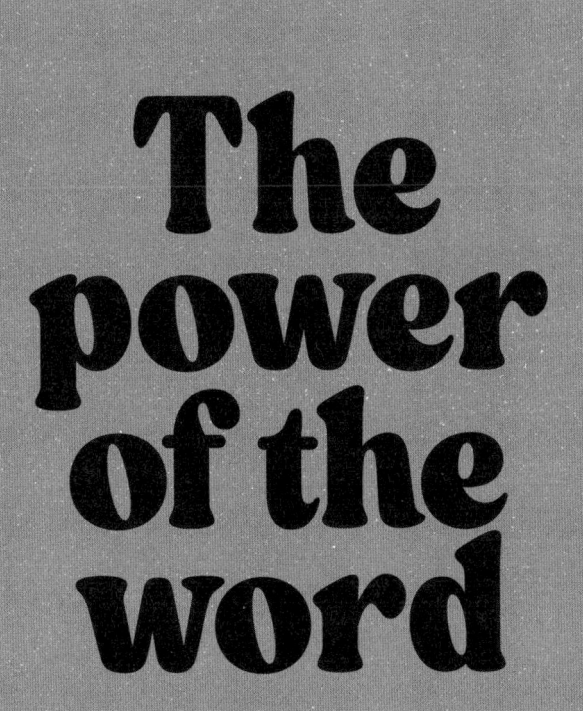

The power of the word

What you say can and will become your reality.

Speak positively.

Your words are literally a vibration and they live on.

What you say can and will become your reality. Do you know people that are always negative and complaining? They're usually creating constant problems for themselves. Their words create negative vibrational patterns.

In fact, a study by researcher Abe Davis at MIT shows how your words can permeate through inanimate objects. Using equipment sensitive enough to record the changes in vibrational frequency of sound currents, the researchers measured how sound actually penetrated inanimate objects and stayed in there. What you say lives in your walls and the structures all around you.

There are physiological, vibrational frequencies permeating into your whole being – your body, your mind, your teeth, your bones – and even your surroundings.

If your words are constantly negative, if you're always complaining, harsh or yelling, or you just have a bad attitude, well, those words have an actual vibration that lives on and on and on.

There is a spiritual teaching: 'Vibrate the cosmos, the cosmos shall clear the path.'

One way to look at this teaching is to keep your sound – your vibe, if you will – at a higher frequency. Loosely speaking, the cosmos is a higher, divine flow of everything. The cosmos is harmony. Use harmonious words, and the cosmos will respond and clear the way.

Several years ago, my wife and I moved into a new apartment. We needed a serious mattress upgrade. We had exhausted our resources on moving expenses, but the mattress was important. I said intently to Jeana, 'We're getting a mattress next week, even if we have to finance it from one of the expensive mattress shops. We are getting a mattress.'

Later that day, one of my very wealthy clients called me and said she had a new mattress sitting in her storage warehouse. It had never been used. She said she had paid over £6,000 ($7,000) for it. Naturally, we said we'd take it. We looked up the mattress online and found it actually cost almost £9,000 ($10,000). My wife and I were blown away.

I declared it. It happened – and it happened in an even better way than I would have expected. Who knew mattresses could cost that much?

Compliment, don't complain

Replace all your complaints with compliments. Alternatively, just don't complain.

Notice people who complain a lot... your friends, family or colleagues. Notice if you're sensitive to it. With many people, a complaint the first thing out of their mouth. It's a buzzkill. If you are being that person, think about what you're creating and the vibration that goes out into the world and how it amplifies. It's like a compound interest of bad vibes. It starts attracting more negativity. It also puts your head in a negative space, where your first reaction is to always complain about something.

This is the same as always focusing on scarcity, right? If you're not in a place of gratitude, then you will often be in a place of lack, and complaining definitely comes from a place of lack. So next time the line is too long, somebody cuts you off in traffic, a cyclist almost runs you over (literally my experience everyday visiting London), or your boss is being annoying, switch your complaint to a compliment.

Do this as casually or as intensely as you like, but the idea is, hey, if we could just start to incorporate some more positivity into our lives, perhaps that will spread and grow.

Be mindful of your words. The main practice here is not to complain. Try it and see how it changes your perspective and outlook on life.

I know someone who incorporated this practice with the intention of becoming a millionaire, and it was something that they adopted passionately.

They are now a millionaire.

Again, did this one practice cause that? No.

Obviously, she had skill in business and other abilities that contributed to her fortune, but the point is that each one of these techniques is a piece in a bigger puzzle. For certain people, certain things might work better than others. She feels that this practice was the one that really shifted things for her.

Even if you fake it in the beginning, even if, internally, you're rolling your eyes, after a while, you will see more of the positive. You will start to see that the universe isn't happening *to* you, but happening *for* you.

I love this teaching: 'Imagine that everything is a conspiracy working in your favour.' This is a fun, light mindset that is meant to open a positive flow of prosperity.

Who wants to be around someone who complains about everything? It's draining, uninteresting and basic. Seriously, it's boring. So, get creative, get complimenting. Turn that frown upside down, and after some time, it will become second nature.

Stop being bothered by every little thing. Your life is bigger than that.

Energy of excuses

Practice •

Consider eliminating these phrases from your vocabulary:

'Yeah, but', 'I can't' **and** *'I can't afford that'.*

'Yeah, but' is a horrible excuse. It crushes possibility. Being riddled with defensive excuses gets you nowhere. It creates friction and disharmony.

When you're building up a defence, it blocks prosperity, because you're basically telling yourself, 'I can't do that.' Then you're always blaming something or someone for why you can't.

If you made a mistake, own up to it. You'll be better for it in the long run.

Words are vibrational patterns that make up sound. The energy of sound goes through your psyche, through your brain and out into other people. It travels across time and space.

What we say and how we say it is important.

I was taught the only thing I can't do is say, 'I can't'. The phrase can really limit possibility and opportunities. If there's something that you really want, be open to it.

Instead of saying 'I can't do it', ask yourself, 'What would it take to do it?' I could climb Mount Everest if I really started getting in shape and decided to pick up mountain climbing, then invested in a guide and dedicated a lot of energy towards it. I am personally not interested enough in climbing Mount Everest to ever undertake that. You get my drift, though: big mountain, big dream. You can.

Lastly, eliminate the phrase 'I can't afford that.'

Instead of focusing on the lack, ask yourself, 'How much is it?' or 'How can I afford it?'

This will shift your mindset to solution-based, practical reality.

Words are important

Practice •

Put your hand on your chest. Speak.
Feel the vibration of your voice. That
vibration is expanding out around
you. Just like your voice carries, your
vibration takes the energy of its intent
and permeates everything. This is
how you create your surroundings;
this is how you create your life.

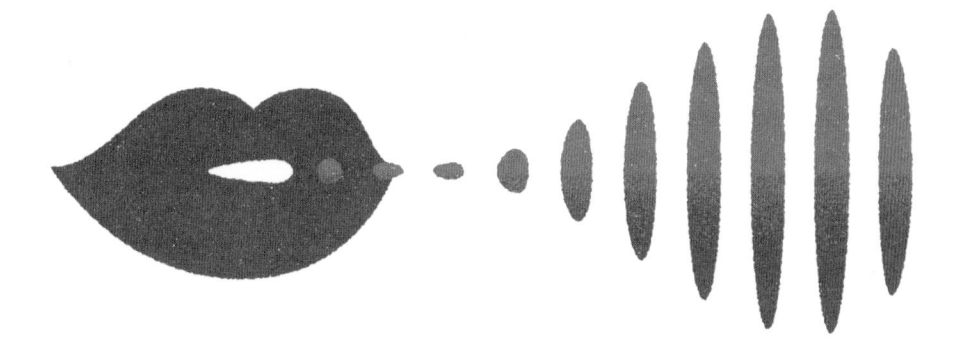

I still love and accept myself

This is an emotional tapping practice that helps release anxiety, fear or whatever you'd like to let go of.

Practice •

Sit in a comfortable position, relax and close your eyes. Let an unresolved issue come into your mind, something that you'd love to be free of. Assess the negative feeling you want to let go of on a scale of one to ten.

I am going to use the example of wanting to shed anxiety over starting a new job.

You would phrase it like this:

'Even though I'm anxious about starting my new job tomorrow, I still love and accept myself.'

As you say your phrase, you will tap nine points on your body with your relaxed fingers. (Look at the diagram on page 68 to see the tapping points.)

Start with the side of your hand below your little finger tapping point (1), repeating the phrase as you tap.

Then move to the next point: the inside of the eyebrow (2).

Still repeating your phrase, move on to the side of the eye (3).

Have conviction and faith in what you are saying. Believe in it.

Pick a goal, like 'I make £200,000 a year,' or 'My haberdashery business makes a million dollars a year.' Whatever your goal is, make it specific to you.

In my experience, I tend to go with things that seem a little bit beyond what seems logical and attainable, and then I work my way up from there. Do not get attached to how the heck it's all going to happen! I know someone who was struggling with their weight. She wanted to lose about 20 kilograms (50 pounds). She decided she would feel the most comfortable at 55 kilograms (120 pounds). She kept saying, 'I need to lose 20 kilograms, I need to lose 20 kilograms,' and nothing was happen. Finally, she started saying this affirmation: 'I weigh 55 kilograms, I weigh 55 kilograms.' Guess how much she weighs now?

This is also about being in the moment and letting it go. Don't overanalyse it, don't overthink it, just do it.

'I am a very successful writer whose books have sold millions of copies.' That's my affirmation.

Have conviction and faith in what you are saying. Believe in it. See it as already existing. It is already written. You need to allow it.

These practices start to create freedom, an ease of life and a synchronicity of success that builds upon success. When we open channels inside ourselves, things start working out a lot better.

Go from a life of feeling like you're always in the wrong place at the wrong time, or a day late and a dollar short, to always being in the right place at the right time, and every situation lining up for you.

You may not have those experiences immediately, but I'll tell you that simply by letting go, easing up and using positive words, you're going to get into a natural flow with affirmations.

Practice •

Speak your affirmations in the present tense as if you've already attained whatever your goal is.

Don't get caught up in how it's going to work out.

Let it flow; allow a sense of ease.

Positive affirmations

Affirmations are words to repeat with an intended goal in mind.

The deeper mystical and yogic teachings cite that the numerology of sound is the number 11 and that the number 11 is infinite, which you can learn more about in my numerology book. There's a teaching that I love that says, 'Fall in love with your sound current.' That sound current is the essence of you. It is your vibration and your frequency, so love it.

When using positive affirmations, state them in the present tense as if you have already succeeded or attained whatever it is you're affirming. This is really important.

Say them out loud or to yourself. But out loud is better.

For example: 'I make over £200,000 a year.' Say it like you have it, even if it isn't true. Believe it.

DO NOT phrase it like this: 'Someday, I will make over £200,000.' Speaking in the future tense is a common mistake with affirmations. If you say it will happen someday, it's always going to be someday.

If you want to have a wonderful, loving relationship with your soulmate, say, 'I have a wonderful, loving relationship with my soulmate,' as opposed to something like, 'I *want* to have a wonderful, loving relationship with my soulmate.'

When I started this journey many years ago, flat broke and coming out of that rock-bottom depression, I found a fortune cookie. It said: 'Next month will be your most profitable month ever.' This was great news, especially at that time in my life. Well, that next month finally arrived, and I looked at that fortune again. It still said, 'Next month will be your most profitable month ever.'

I see this mistake often with affirmations and positive thinking.

Even if you don't physically have it or emotionally have it, always speak it in the present tense: 'I am having my most profitable month ever.'

Repeat while tapping under the eye (4).

Then move the tapping to under your nose (5).

Repeat on your chin (6).

Repeat on your collarbone (7).

Repeat under your armpits (8).

Repeat on the top of your head (9), the ninth and final spot.

Now assess the strength of the negative feeling once more (in this example, anxiety), rating it from one to ten. It should be lower than when you started the exercise.

Go through all nine tapping points again, but this time shorten the phrase.

For this example: 'Even though new job, I still love and accept myself.'

Once completed, assess how you're feeling on a scale of one to ten once more.

If negative feelings are still lingering, you can do it again, but shorten the phrase still further.

For this example, just say: 'job'.

The idea is to get your negative feelings down to one if you can. If not one, the goal is to at least manage a less stressful feeling than when you started.

The first time I did this, I closed my eyes and recalled an argument that my parents had at the top of the stairs in our house when I was about seven years old. It was a typical household argument, but for some reason it was still anxiously lingering inside of me. When I let go and I allowed it to come to the surface, I said,

'Okay, even though my parents had a huge argument on top of the stairs, I still love and accept myself.' Eventually, after working through the nine tapping points and reducing it down to a few words, I released tension that I didn't even know my body and mind were still carrying after all these years.

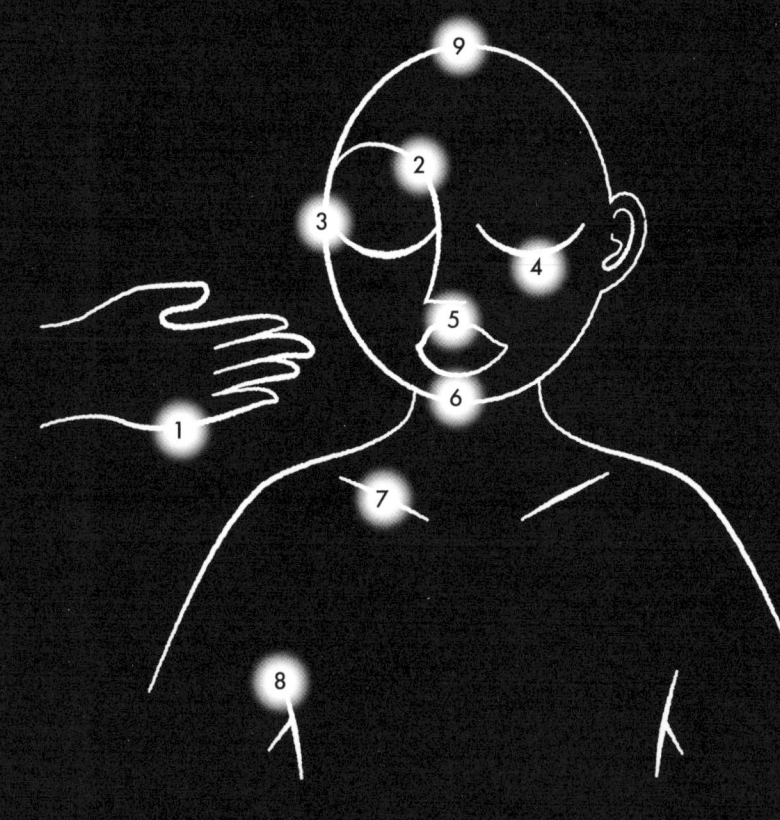

Victory

The word 'victory' is a very powerful mantra and can be used as a really simple practice.

Practice •

Say the word 'victory'.

Whether you're working on a project, interviewing for a new job, applying to a new school – whatever it is, the practice is to 'chant' the word victory. 'Victory, victory, victory, victory, victory.'

You can say it as many times as you like, out loud or to yourself. Whatever works for you. The spiritual teaching is to use 108 repetitions. It is even used as a mantra in some yogic practices.

Your full financial wish list

Practice •

Write an unfiltered list of every financial goal you have. It doesn't matter how big or how small, just write a list. Don't hold back. Don't edit, don't censor yourself, don't feel ashamed. Enjoy it. Feel empowered and go big.

I had so many things on my list the first time I did this. One of the most important was being financially solvent enough to provide my mother with a little house where she could garden. I wanted her to be well taken care of.

Then it happened.

Here's the point of this story: I did not buy my mom a house, although that would've been really cool. What I did do was write it on my financial wish list as an intention. About a year later, she called me and told me that she had met somebody; everything was moving fast, he was a wonderful man and they were getting married. I was very surprised and happy for her. My father died many years ago, so this was all very exciting.

Her new partner is a wonderful guy. He bought them a great little house with mountain views where they spend their days gardening. It's exactly what she wanted. And it's what I envisioned for her, only better.

The moral of this story is: sometimes you never know.

It's important to have a vision and it's even more important to stay open to something better and unexpected.

I mean this very humbly. I'm not taking credit (maybe just a little), but I really believe in my heart of hearts that putting that intention down started something. On some level, it was my prayer for her.

I'm sorry.
Please forgive me.
Thank you.
I love you.

Some years ago, a friend of mine from Hawaii taught me this beautiful practice.

I was feeling really upset and worried about the future ('future-tripping' as we call it) while also regretting all my past decisions because I liked to be hard on myself for all the opportunities I had missed and the mistakes I had made. I was feeling a lot of fear about what was coming next. I didn't have enough, I wouldn't ever have enough; I just wasn't going to make it. Basically, it was a normal day for me back then.

My Hawaiian friend asked me to sit with my eyes closed and put my left hand over my heart centre (which is the centre of your upper chest, not your biological heart). With my right hand over my left, I closed my eyes, took a deep breath and repeated these words after her: 'I'm sorry. Please forgive me. Thank you. I love you.'

I took a breath and she had me say it again. 'I'm sorry. Please forgive me. Thank you. I love you.'

I said that over and over again for about 5 minutes, maybe longer. She didn't instruct any length of time. I opened my eyes, and that was it. It was beautiful.

Practice •

Try it.

'I'm sorry.
Please forgive me.
Thank you.
I love you.
I'm sorry.
Please forgive me.
Thank you.
I love you.'

Manifestation list

Practice •

For this practice, make a manifestation list of your goals, and be specific as to how these goals will be met.

What happens in vagueness, stays in vagueness. So be specific.

For example, let's you have a business and you provide a service. Whatever your business is, state your financial goal and that you'll make that money through that business.

Maybe you're a writer, and you want to be a bestselling author and worth millions of dollars. You need to say that: 'I've made millions of dollars with my bestselling books.'

You need to have a vehicle, a container for goals or money to come through. I personally did this when manifesting a new home. I made a list of what I wanted. I knew I needed a space for an office, room for our child, room to grow and a guest room. We wanted a media area separate from our living room, et cetera, et cetera. We were specific.

If you're making financial goals on this manifestation list, it's really important to get clear on *how* that money is going to come in.

Don't just say, 'Oh, I want to have a lot of money.' Instead, be specific: 'I make millions of dollars with my potato chip company or my tea company.' Whatever the goal is, that's up to you – that's your business.

This doesn't just apply to financial goals. Whatever it is that you're trying to manifest, state how it will be achieved. For example, you might think: 'I want to be very successful.' Okay, well, what does that mean? Perhaps you've just graduated law school. So you want to be a very, very successful lawyer. Once you have your list, read it out loud before you go to bed; let it be the last thing you see before you close your eyes. When you get up in the morning, read that list again. This list can be as big or as small as you like.

The 'yes' practice

It's very easy to get into a routine of saying no. Whether you actually say the word or not, it is a 'no' attitude that limits possibility, miracles and opportunities. Bigger things can happen; we don't necessarily know why or how.

If things feel stale, stuck or resistant to change, say yes. Sometimes you just need to say yes to clear the obstacles. Get out of your comfort zone by doing something you haven't done. Yes, yes, yes.

Practice •

For this exercise, say 'yes' while you reach your arms up to the sky as if you're receiving a blessing. Keep doing it. Try it for 3 minutes. You can do it for less time, or you can do it for longer.

Each time you say 'yes', stretch out your arms and reach to the heavens, reach to the sky, then bring your arms back to your chest. When you say 'yes' again, reach to the sky once more. 'Yes, yes, yes, yes.' That's it.

See how you feel after doing that for 3 minutes. Heck, do it just for 1 minute. Get used to this frequency in your brain. Condition this affirmative language and get better at starting to go for it, whatever *it* is for you.

Get out of your comfort zone by doing something you haven't done.

Just say no

Sometimes, using the word no is just as hard, if not harder, than saying yes.

You can experience a lot of freedom in your life when you say no to something you know you don't want or don't want to do. It's okay to just say no.

When you know, you no.

This is similar to the 'yes' practice on page 76. Instead of saying yes, we say NO.

Practice •

Sit or stand in a comfortable position. Take your arms and criss-cross them over your body, pointing them down at a 45-degree angle. Then swing them back and forth, criss-crossing them almost like a pair of scissors pointing down, and just say, 'No, no, no, no.'

It's very liberating. When you get comfortable saying no, it's a lot easier to stand up for yourself. You realise after a while it's no big deal to say no and you're not offending people. You're not hurting people. You're just not interested. It's great.

Remember, NO is a complete sentence.

- **Your words can and will become your reality, so choose them and use them wisely.**

- **Avoid the negativity that comes with complaining and excuses, and embrace the positivity of affirmations, self-acceptance and powerful language.**

- **Harness the power of manifestation.**

- **Take control of 'yes' and 'no'.**

Part three:

Let go to grow

This is about clearing the way, clearing the space.

This is about letting go of the old. Letting go of the past. Letting go of useless identities, old behaviours, old routines. Letting go of those tired and worn-out parts of your life. These can be physical items, emotions, thoughts, relationships. It's about giving yourself a clean slate, a fresh start. It's time to be free.

Abundance is ready to show up if you just get out of the way. Clear the blocks.

These practices help. Creating space allows for more opportunity, for more prosperity, for more abundance. It's impossible to fill a full cup. These practices are about letting go. Physical, emotional and mental clutter can take up a lot of space in your life. Physical clutter takes up space in your house, in your car. Emotional clutter takes up space in your heart and your relationships. Mental clutter takes up space in your head and your communications.

We all know how good it feels to have a nice, clean, fresh, new, clear space. That's what all of this is about. It's creating headspace, heart space, physical space. Getting rid of the old. These are opportunities to examine what isn't meant to be any more. Accept that the time has come to renew in order to be you.

This is about liberation, freedom, lightness of being, manoeuvrability and opportunity. Lighten the load. No more baggage. There's an old Egyptian teaching that when one was judged, it was to determine if one's heart was as light as a feather. What makes your heart heavy? What makes your head heavy? What makes your life heavy? What feels sluggish, slow and inert?

It's time to clear the way. Become a fit receptacle; create the container that will hold the blessings.

Get rid of at least one item a day

Practice •

Unload at least one physical item every single day.

This is an opportunity to clear out, declutter, reorganise, rearrange and let go of dead weight in your life.

How much can you get rid of?

Everybody has things they could get rid of. When we did this with the Prosperity Family collective, many people shared that they cleared vanloads of stuff. They gave it away to charity. They sent it to second-hand shops for resale. However you want to get rid of your stuff, that is up to you.

Clearing your physical space clears your headspace.

The outer world affects your inner world, and your inner world affects your outer world.

I hear so many stories about people who are single and really want to attract a partner, and it often turns out that they, literally and figuratively, do not have the space for one. For example, maybe their bed is up against the wall and only

accessible on one side, because it's more convenient. Maybe they've had the same old sheets for the last five years. Maybe their car passenger seat is full of papers and old water bottles and other clutter. Where's the room for a partner?

Physical stuff holds vibration and creates emotional clutter. Getting rid of things that no longer serve you is a wonderful way to begin to free yourself up. Just let go.

How do you expect to attract new, better opportunities if you're holding on to the stale old past?

You probably have books that you will never read, shoes that are worn out, an ex-partner's shirt or something that is no longer serving you.

Everyone has a junk drawer. Even a minimalist can find things they could get rid of.

Once you start to clear the space around you, you may find resentment, sorrow,

regret, stagnation... (I could go on, but you get the idea) hidden in your physical, emotional and mental.

The first time I started going through the usual clutter, with the aim of getting rid of buttons from old shirts that I knew I would never sew on, old soy sauce and ketchup bottles and plastic takeaway utensils, when halfway through lightening my load I got a letter in the mail from a law firm in San Francisco with a check for £1,300 ($1,500). Unbeknownst to me, I had been listed in a class-action lawsuit from an old employer, and had been awarded that money.

I ended up using it on a wonderful little getaway for my wife's birthday. We went to a new city we had never been to, stayed in a really nice hotel and ate foods we had never tried before. I was grateful. So I spent it on someone who inspires me to feel grateful every day. Plus, it was nice to splurge more than we would have usually spent. I'm convinced

it came about because of me clearing out dead energy, likely the soy sauce from 2019.

It is freeing and it is liberating. It's also very nice to have a clean, clear, bright and free space for opportunity to come through. Empty your cup so you can fill it with something new, vibrant and fresh. Remember, we are creating space to receive gifts and blessings.

Again, all of you will have your own experience with this practice. Letting go of physical clutter helps us let go of other issues. For many people, it turns into a deep emotional transformation. It churns them out of resentment and being attached to old ideals – i.e. old parts of themselves.

One person I knew, who really identified as being a punk rocker, shifted to another set of ideals after doing this practice. She'd been holding on to a leather jacket for years that she didn't wear.

It was something that she had spent a lot of money on. She couldn't justify letting it go, but when she did, it totally freed her from an identity that no longer fit with who she was. Soon after that she met a partner who was aligned with who she had allowed herself to grow into. It was a beautiful thing.

Was it that one coat? I don't know, but she believes that by clearing out space for her, she just happened to clear out an old identity, too. She still enjoys punk music but she grew and she changed. I have had old identities and things that I have had to let go of, too. I don't play with children's toys any more. I don't have toy fire trucks and Lego. But now that I have a son, all of that will probably show up in my life in a new way.

Try it. Let go. And let go of your attachment to the result. Don't do it with a specific goal in mind. Observe what happens. Let go to grow.

Empty your cup so you can fill it with something new, vibrant and fresh.

Best foot forwards

Practice •

Clean your shoes.

Many years ago, I had a roommate who came from a troubled past. He had been involved in a very tough Los Angeles street gang. He spent many years in prison and, while he definitely looked like someone you wouldn't want to meet in a dark alley, he was the sweetest, greatest, nicest guy. He helped a lot of people, many men in particular, get out of that lifestyle, straighten up, get great jobs and become very productive members of society.

The thing that I learned the most from him was how to keep a very clean Zen space. He loved sneakers. At the end of every day, he would clean the edges of his shoes with a little cleaner to get all the scuff marks off.

I noticed how brilliantly clean and shiny all his shoes were, and it only took him a few minutes at the end of the day. So, I started doing it too. I liked letting go of the dirt; it physically cleared up our living space and made me feel good. Cleanliness made me feel bright, made me feel smart and made me feel fresh. Respecting my shoes rippled out to a deeper respect for myself.

I've always cherished this lesson. He was a wise teacher. His personal transformation is inspiring and hopeful. Sometimes it's the little things, like clean shoes that make the biggest difference.

Know your worth

How much are you getting paid?
Is it worth it? Are you worth it?

Practice •

Sit in a place where it is safe to get into a
meditative state. Close your eyes. Meditate on
what you're currently offering people. What are
you actually giving and doing? Go deep into it,
and now ask yourself, what is it really worth? If
money wasn't an object, how much would you
pay for it? Now assess its worth and compare it
to how much you're charging or getting paid.

You can apply this to your job, your
business, etc. What do you offer? What
is your work? What is that worth?

There is a teaching that says, 'State
your worth and that shall be it.'

Another one is, 'Invoice the universe.'

Learn to stand up for what you're truly worth
and what your value is. Standing up for yourself,
asking for a pay rise, being realistic or realising
that you're in a position where maybe you could
be worth more, may open up channels for you
to create more opportunities in your life.

Show the world how expansive you can
be and try asking for your worth.

Tracking numbers

Money matters. It is okay to be devoutly spiritual and have a prosperous financial life. I believe that spirituality is the whole of your life and that money is a very significant part of that. Our societies have a lot of issues around money: money is seen as evil, not spiritual; in fact, it's often considered the antithesis of spirituality. There's so much maladaptive conditioning around finance. On the yogic ashram where I grew up, there was a select group of people who took very intense monastic vows, which basically meant they gave up earthly possessions of any kind, including money. It was a vow of celibacy and dedication to spiritual pursuit.

As a child, I perceived that noble pursuits are the highest spiritual quest and that money was only a distraction from that. As I grew up, however, I found many different teachers, traditions and practices that teach that money is absolutely a part of our lives. I needed to let go of that personal conditioning. It took me some time to get the drive, but money has given me so many more options and so much more opportunity.

Making more money has been life-changing in so many ways. I see how being broke was for me inadvertently selfish. I couldn't give to myself or anyone else. Financial solvency is one of the biggest anxiety relievers of all time.

It creates stability and security.

I'm giving you permission to say, 'Hey, it's completely okay to make money.

It's okay to make a lot of money.

It's okay to be completely prosperous.'

Money creates freedom. So, let go of any narratives around money being the root of all evil, and any beliefs that money can only be earned through excruciating hard work. Of course, you should definitely apply effort, gumption and diligence. Offer a quality service and/or products. Act honestly and sincerely. We all have the right to do well. If you adopt this approach, success is inevitable.

Practice •

Keep track of your numbers.

Use a notebook, spreadsheet or app to help you keep track of the money coming in and going out.

This is not about accounting. This is not about creating budgets. I prefer not to use the word 'budget'. I suggest using the phrase 'spending plan'. 'Budget' holds the energy of cutting corners; it's about what you're *not* allowed to do. Whereas the notion of a 'spending plan' lights up all the YES channels in your brain. Yes is going to help you get to where you want to be. You're giving yourself permission and structure.

Start tracking your numbers. Every time you earn money, record how much comes in. Even if you find money on the street, log that. Everything that comes in, keep track of it. Make a note of every pound you spend and what you spent it on (for example: groceries: £50, coffee: £5.75, gift: £25). It isn't about accounting. When this was taught to me, I was told that this helps your brain open up other channels. Don't ask, just do.

Get a handle on money. Know your numbers.

Save at least three months' worth of living expenses in a savings account.

When I was able to glance at my accounts easily and know, 'I have this amount of dollars, I've spent this amount of dollars,' the guilt and fear dropped away. It was a relief to know what I had. This is the prosperity of clarity. I'm ashamed to admit that I was the guy who would make a £10 ($12) purchase and have no idea if my card would get declined. Every time I went shopping was a ridiculous game of Russian roulette. This was all rooted in my fear of money, which, at the time, was really just a fear of lack. I was scared to confront the reality of what I had – or didn't have.

When I started doing this, I was amazed. Things shifted very quickly. I started to live more honestly and openly. Just by keeping track of my numbers.

It reminds me of that old saying, 'It takes money to make money.' I always thought it meant you needed money to make more money. But becoming more cognisant of the amount of money coming in and the amount of money going out, and looking at that number daily (sometimes several times a day), somehow created more money. It was fascinating and amazing. For me, this was one of the biggest life-changing practices.

Save money out of trust. Not out of fear. Trust that you can put money aside because you're going to keep making more of it.

Having savings is a wonderful luxury.

I was taught to always have money set aside so that you can live the lifestyle that you're living now for the next three months without earning another dollar. This seemed impossible to me at a time when I was doing odd jobs, like on-demand grocery delivery, occasional readings for a few clients and working in a health-food store. I was definitely hustling, but I was also shocked that, within a few months of tracking my numbers I had set aside three months' worth of funds.

This is the prosperity of clarity.

Get clear and get honest with yourself. Let go of the fear.

Be specific.

When my wife and I were looking to buy a house, we really had no idea what we were doing. We had no clue how much we would need or how much we would qualify for if we tried for a loan.

But we had been saving money knowing that we would need it for a down payment, the move, plus everything else. We got clear and learned what we had to do.

The point is: whatever your goal is, be specific.

Once we knew how much money we could borrow, we then knew what our price range was. From there, we assessed, 'Okay, how much do we need for a down payment, and how much do we need for closing costs?' The specificity absolutely helped us manifest. We got clear and, voilà, we did it!

Knowing your numbers will manifest more money.

When you have the courage to know specifically how much you need for something, the right channels will open up. Remember say, 'How much will it cost?' not 'I can't afford it.'

Forgive yourself. Move out of regret: 'I wasted all this money going out,' or 'I bought a ridiculous car.' The list goes on. Remember to start where you're at.

If you can use this practice to honestly assess what you have and to stop fearing what you don't have, you can confront the reality of the situation without getting worked up or judging yourself.

None of this will change completely overnight, but keep doing it. I chipped away at it, day by day, and here I am. I went from earning £9.70 ($11) an hour to hundreds of thousands a year doing what I love the most.

Always be earning

If you're asking the universe for money, show the universe you mean business.

Practice •

Do things that earn you money. Even if it's working a job that you don't care about or something extra on the side. Tell yourself that this is part of your growth. Earning money is a form of self-love and self-care. Making more money will change your life.

When you are asking, praying or setting intentions for more money and the opportunity shows up for you to make that money, don't shun it. You will short-circuit the situation. You will short-circuit your mind. Here you are, telling your mind and the universe one thing, then doing the opposite.

We've all done jobs that aren't our biggest, most dream-fulfilling occupations. That's okay. Sometimes the goal is just the money. If you need money, then it's no big deal. Be nice to yourself about it. You're taking care of yourself to the best of your ability in the moment. You're in a good flow, even if it doesn't seem like it on paper. As you put energy towards earning money, it grows more money. It tells the universe that you're out there wanting to make money and in turn more opportunities will show up.

If money happens to be one of your big goals, the simple philosophy is to always be earning. All these practices open you up to bigger opportunities of all kinds. I've certainly done a million jobs that, at the time, definitely didn't feel like my destiny, but when I got the money, I started to put it aside to utilise it for my destiny.

Money is a tool to enhance your life and your destiny. It's not always about how you get it. Don't discriminate. Act with reverence and self-respect. Don't be above work, it's a bad attitude and an energy-blocker.

Approach every job as an act of service. No matter what. You've agreed to do it, so do it well. Do it with excellence. Have you noticed it's a lot easier to get a job when you already have a job? So, even if you want another job, you're going to change the energy by continuing to do the job that you have now, and doing it well, even if your ego doesn't like it. Love it, do it, do it as an act of service and do it to the best of your ability.

50 things you can do to earn money now

If you're feeling unsure where to make changes financially, or if you're falling into lack and scarcity, obsessed with everything you don't have, or you just want to make some more money, this is a practice for you.

Practice •

Simply write down 50 things you could do right now to earn more money. That's it. If you come up with more, that's great, but capture at least 50.

These may be things that you never actually do, but that you could do. Write them down nonetheless. Maybe you could help clean houses, collect scrap metal, set up a lemonade stand, pet-sit or consult for Fortune 500 companies. The idea is to open your mind to more possibilities and see how capable you are. Just dive in: don't worry about it. Don't worry if it's something you could never do, like dig ditches. I'm sure you could if you had to and maybe there's an opportunity there.

The idea is to get it on paper to see how many skills you have and what your talents are. It's a great practice for moving away from 'freaking out' about not having enough or thinking that your options are very limited. Historically, there's never been as much opportunity to earn extra money as there is today. From gigs and industry apps to hobbies and online stores, the list goes on. So, leave it up to your imagination and get going.

Magnify your money

Every time you give money, or pay
for goods and services, bless it. Bless
where it's going. Bless where it may
land. Imagine the good that it is doing.
Remind yourself that it's leaving you
to increase your prosperity 10 times,
100 times, maybe more. Feel good
about it. Be grateful that you had it.

Meditation

One of the benefits of meditation is to cleanse the subconscious.

This is how to clean your brain. The truth is, sometimes we all need a little 'brainwashing'. It will put you in a more peaceful and calm state than when you started. My personal experience is that meditation makes me feel good, and when I feel good, I interact with the world with a much better attitude. Things just don't bother me as much.

Take time to get centred and clear your mind. This is an internal process that greatly affects your outer world.

I don't wish to impose any particular tradition or spiritual practice on you. You may already be meditating! I would certainly encourage you to explore the different techniques you are drawn to.

Practice •

For our purposes, start with 11 minutes of mind-stilling. Do this at any time of day. Sit in a comfortable position. Close your eyes for 11 minutes. Do your best to let go and think of nothing.

Part of this practice is to let go. Don't worry about what comes up. Don't analyse it. Don't beat yourself up if you're overthinking, if you're processing something, if you've had a bad day, or dwelling on an argument with your spouse, or you're still mentally giving the finger to that guy who cut you off in traffic... the list will always go on: that's why we're here. Take 11 minutes, close your eyes, relax your breath, and sit in that calm space. Don't complicate it.

Conscious breathing

Breathwork is one of the fastest ways to get centred, become calmer and more empowered, and release feelings of worry, stress and anxiety. The yogic teaching is that our breath is prana and prana is the life force of the universe. Scientifically speaking, breath gives you more oxygen. More oxygen gives you more vitality. Vitality is life. By breathing consciously you become even more alive.

Esoterically speaking, breath gives you more prana. More prana gives you more power, and more power allows you to easily manoeuvre through time and space.

There are countless breath practices out there. In yogic technology, it is recommended that if you don't do anything else, at least do 11 minutes of conscious breathwork a day. Keep it simple. Pause to take a few deep breaths and relax.

Here is a simple breathing exercise.

Practice • Three-part 1-minute breath

Sit in a comfortable position. Take a slow, deep inhale for a count of 20 seconds. Hold your breath for 20 seconds, then exhale for 20 seconds.

Start out with a few minutes. Feel free to incorporate this into the mind-stilling meditation.

You're also welcome to cut the time if needed. For example, a 10-second inhale, 10-second hold and 10-second exhale or 5/5/5.

What's important is equal breathing. If you practise this, you will get better at it over time.

The accountability loose-ends list

This practice creates practical change while clearing a lot of headspace.

Practice •

Make a list of all the loose ends in your life. Write everything down, as much as you can remember. It could be something as minuscule as replacing the screw of your silverware drawer handle, or dusting behind your dresser. It could be as major as organising a move to another country, paying back taxes, starting a business, getting your website up to date or starting a class-action lawsuit against the government for crimes against humanity. It doesn't matter how big or how small the task is – the point is to write it all down. Everything you've been sweeping under the rug, everything you're avoiding – get it on the page.

Once you have your entire list in place, start checking something off every day.

Beyond its obvious practicality, taking the time to write down and look at everything that is taking up space in your head or keeping you up at night will liberate you. This is accountability gold.

Start getting things done. Make a commitment. Hold yourself accountable. Maybe multiply your accountability by doing this in a group. Pick a couple of friends or one other person and check in habitually. It can be daily or weekly in whatever format you like (phone call, text, email or public forum, etc.) and share what you have accomplished that day.

The key is to avoid judgement. You may get a lot done in one day, you may get nothing done, but when you check in, even if it's to say, 'Hey, you know what, I didn't do anything,' it's important that you don't make excuses or judge your peers. By showing up for yourself and others, you will open up a lot of channels.

My experience with this has been that these little undone things turn into bigger things. The more I check off, the freer I begin to feel, as if I didn't realise how much underlying stress was eating away at me. For me, procrastination causes so much stress, but what I'm most stressed about are the things I put off doing. It's a futile cycle. Remember the teaching: 'There is a way through every block.'

Examine all the things that may be keeping you up at night without you knowing. If they're not keeping you up at night, more power to you, but they're taking up space in your life as indolence. Clear them out. If you're clogged with all these little tasks to address, you won't have room for new opportunities. That's the heart of letting go to grow. Create the physical space, the headspace, the emotional space, the heart space to be more expansive and allow more opportunities.

I had a spiritual teacher for many years who always said, 'If you can't get your sock drawer organised, how do you expect your destiny to give you bigger, better opportunities?' It's like that old saying, 'Chop wood, carry water.' Small, consistent, mundane tasks lead to greater, expansive growth. Organise your sock drawer. These little things, like fixing the tiniest loose screw, can lead to bigger things, like starting a class-action lawsuit against your government. It's going to feel good to get the momentum going.

Make a vision board

This is a great technique for programming your mind. I've heard countless first-hand stories of houses imagined then secured, goals met, and visual representations chosen with intuition that have opened into miraculous real-life experiences.

A vision board is a collage of aspirations, i.e. things you want your life to include. It's something that you look at daily as a reminder to your subconscious mind, conscious mind and your higher self. The more your mind sees what it wants, the more it consciously and unconsciously begins to open up ways to make those opportunities happen. Some say it opens up a channel for higher forces or for more beneficence to work in your favour. How you think it is working is less important than doing it well and seeing it work.

Let loose, go a little bigger than you imagined is possible and just see where it goes.

Practice •

The traditional way to do this is to get your hands on some old magazines, photos and picture books. All things that you can cut up. You'll need a large piece of paper or poster board to arrange them on, and then you can start gluing.

There's no size regulation, formation, or any rules. Just choose things that inspire you, things that you like, things that you are drawn to, plus your goals and aspirations in images or words. Personally, I really like using words, but you can use words and visuals – mix and match. What's really important is that you do you and don't hold back.

Have a vision-board party. Ask your guests to bring old magazines, books, stationery and scissors, or use a vision board app – yes, they exist. If you're great at Photoshop, more power to you; just get together in the name of prosperity and enjoy one another's company as you bring your dreams into reality.

I made a vision board on my phone, because I figured my phone is probably the thing I look at the most. Every time I checked the time, every time there was an alert, my subconscious got to see everything I was working to attract into my life. Years ago, I made a vision board of goals and aspirations; nearly all of it has come true. For example, I added the words 'world traveller', along with a picture of a little aeroplane that I liked. Since then, I have had the opportunity to teach and travel all over the world.

Not only that, but I made it before I had any consistent income to speak of. I put down financial goals that felt unattainable. I actually thought, 'Oh, well, maybe this is too high.' Yet today, I have more than surpassed that amount. It's probably time for me to do another vision board with a much higher amount.

Don't be afraid. Don't hold back.

Before I got my first book deal, I wrote 'number-one bestseller' thinking, 'Maybe I will write a book.' My book *Numerology* was a number-one bestseller on Amazon in many different categories before it was even released. I suppose it's time for a *New York Times* bestseller image.

I have made vision boards in the past with imagery of being in a beautiful, wonderful relationship and marriage. I had a vision board with a home, which literally seemed impossible, yet here I am writing this book from the home that I own with my wife – who herself was the pinnacle of one of my vision boards way before I ever met her.

These things work. I've heard countless stories from people who find an old vision board and see that every single thing has come to fruition. Have fun with it.

The lunar calendar: new moon, full moon

Tracking the cycles of the new moon and the full moon is a great way to get into a natural flow. In my spiritual tradition we do a lot of work to align ourselves with nature. The flow of the earth extends to the cosmos and allows for clean, holistic and more natural living. Even if you don't believe in astrology, you can still use these phases of the moon as prompts to do certain practices.

The new moon is a time to start something new.

The idea behind this is that: once the moon is new, it reaches a zero point, a clean slate. After that point, the moon starts to wax, meaning that it is is growing. You're working with this momentum, so flow with the grow. Even if it's just symbolic for you, why not embrace it? Start something new, just to try it.

Plant seeds for new projects and new beginnings, and set intentions. This is a really good time to write new positive affirmations and utilise these prosperity practices. Then, as the moon grows, you get into a wonderful flow.

The full moon is the time to shed, to let go.

Just as the moon is getting full, we reach a pinnacle of energy. Whichever practice you put into action at the new moon has grown to its potential for this cycle. Right after the moon is full, it wanes and begins to diminish. It's shedding. It's letting go. What can you shed during this time?

Note: it is essential to start your new moon practices and intentions right when the moon is new, or just after, so you're in the space of the moon growing. If you set these intentions the day before the new moon is new, when it's still waning, they will be cancelled energetically or conceptually.

Though I love looking at the moon and the moon's cycles, I am not hard-nosed about it. Sometimes life moves, and you've got to start something when you've got to start. We don't always have the luxury of starting on a new moon or a full moon, it's just something to be aware of that will enhance these practices and may open up some other ideas, energies and philosophies.

Have fun with it! The moon represents your inner self as well as your subconscious. The idea is to get much more in touch with your authenticity and clear any energy to allow for a pure, meaningful, unique space.

Practice •

New moon:

A time for new projects, new intentions, positive affirmations. It's a good time to start one of the practices in this book, such as writing your financial wish list (page 70).

Full moon:

It's time to give things away. This is a wonderful time for letting go to grow, practising forgiveness and releasing resentments.

Change it up

Do something new every day.

As the saying goes, change is the only constant.

Do you know what trouser (pant) leg you put on first? What shoe do you put on first? Chances are, you probably had to think about that for a second. How much of our lives are spent in an unconscious pattern of inertia? If you're not aware, then who is? If you don't have a vision for yourself, someone or something else will decide for you.

This practice is intended to break the spell of the sluggish rut. If you're feeling like your life is the same crap just on a different day, then this is one for you. It's fun and easy.

Simply try something new every day. It could be a new food, or maybe you've been taking exactly the same route to work every day for the last five years, so try a different commute. Rearrange the furniture of your home and your brain. Wear a colour you never wear. Learn a new skill, try out a new hobby. If you're right-handed, try using your left hand more, or vice versa. The possibilities are literally endless.

This practice also helps you adapt better to changes, and when you can adapt to change, it's easier to seize opportunities.

Be spontaneous, have a great time and let loose.

Resentment

Resentment is drinking the poison and expecting the other person to die.

Resentment is powerful. Resentment brings people down. Resentment is a major reason that we sabotage, self-sabotage and create a lot of conflict in life.

Resentments keep us small and angry, and make us frustrated, trapped or oppressed in some way. Whether legitimate or imagined, the feeling is real.

We're all going to experience it in different ways, and it may manifest differently with different personalities.

My personal experience with resentment is usually frustration. It happens when I feel as though something isn't being taken care of properly, or if something or someone is taking advantage of me or thwarting an opportunity. It makes me angry. I get SO [insert harsh expletive of your choosing] frustrated dealing with big corporations where you can't get a human being on the phone to have a rational conversation. For example, booking a hotel, then needing to cancel the reservation. All these companies use the smokescreen of the internet

and more than one customer services so you can never speak to a manager or anyone who has a vested interest in the company. When you finally give up and you can't cancel a £300 ($386) reservation, even though there was a huge blizzard and the wedding you were going to was cancelled and the hotel was shut, you just got screwed. This happened to me a few years ago and I'm still angry and resentful. Resentful enough to be writing a page in a book about it. Clearly, I need to do another round of this practice. At the end of the day, I need to remind myself that if a £300 hotel reservation is my biggest problem, then I'm doing quite well – and I can also remember that at one point, I was living off food stamps worth £170 ($190) a month.

The point is, resentment can show up no matter what your life is like on the outside. So much resentment comes from the inability to speak up for yourself and/or take action for yourself.

Practise speaking up. So many resentments start small and go unaddressed until they've become huge, festering problems.

The toilet seat that is never put down, the cabinet door that is never closed, the teapot full of swollen loose tea in the sink (I'm hoping my wife reads this). That coworker on your team who's always late. I could go on and on. You get the point.

If you don't speak up, your feelings can billow to the point that you're deeply angry, and that is when you may lash out. Big or small, it comes down to bottled-up resentment.

Resentment is a tool of the dark side. We've seen horrible things play out in the world because of it. If you step back and examine it, so much is because of resentment.

Look at Darth Vader's story from *Star Wars*. He was a spiritual warrior monk in training. He was one of the good guys. When his teacher wouldn't let him use magic (aka the Force) to rescue his mother, he went dark. He turned on his people. He turned on the galaxy. He became Mr Evil, and it all started because of resentment. On some level, this is what's going on within each of us.

So, let's start to clear some of this.

Practice •

Write down a resentment.

How does it make you feel?

How would you like this to be resolved differently?

Rewrite the scenario, imagining how you would have liked it to play out in a more positive way.

Make a list on paper (this is important and will make sense at the end) of all the resentments you can think of, no matter how big or small. It can be as small as that kid who cut in line for the swing when you were eight years old, or it could be as big as getting dumped by the love of your life.

The point is, it's still in there somewhere if you're thinking about it. I'm still thinking about the time this kid stole my lunch in sixth grade. I'm also laughing about it, because I was raised by hippy vegetarians, and it was a tofu sandwich. Honestly, I wouldn't be surprised if it had nutritional yeast on it. This was tofu in the 1980s, before anyone knew about it in Western culture. Except, of course, vegetarian hippies who also enjoyed eating yeast. The poor kid ate a tofu sandwich. I guess, in the end, revenge was mine. But... all joking aside, this is an example of something being held on to. This is an example of my desire for revenge. It's not healthy. Resentment will keep you down.

As you make this list, just write down everything that comes up. When you feel like you're done and you've got it all down, spend a few quiet moments with yourself. Then, if you have the space to do this safely, read through the list and then burn it. This is a ritual. Burn off the resentments so they no longer burn you. You may find that it's not even about the specific resentment, it's that resentment is a go-to response and a habit. Let's free ourselves from this negative pattern.

Media cleanse

Try cleansing your life of all media — social media, news, television shows, etc.

Figure out a time frame for this and stick to it.

In this day and age, even one day would be helpful.

Cleansing yourself of social media and the news will make the biggest difference.

I'm part of a spiritual tradition that teaches us to never watch the news. When it was taught to me, it was 'Never read a newspaper.' Yes, I'm that old. Trust me, you'll know what you need to know if it's up close and personal.

For almost everyone, most news you're consuming and getting worked up about has no bearing on your life, and it isn't something which you have any control over. Sure, there's always an exception.

I can almost guarantee if you tried this for even a week, you'll see you didn't miss out on anything. Also, people seem to forget that 'the news' is sometimes for profit and entertainment. I'm a self-confessed media junkie. I scroll through way too much news. I use social media to promote my work, I podcast, I create teaching videos and I write books. When I do this, I focus on creating content and moving on. I know many of us have jobs in media and it can be impossible to avoid it entirely.

Do your best to consume less. Take time to learn a new skill, go exploring, or meet up with a friend or family member. Who cares what Harry Styles and Arianna Grande are doing, or what world leaders are having for dinner? All this media just becomes clutter in the mind. It's wise to give it a rest once in a while. Clean your screen.

- Let go of what no longer works for you in order to create new headspace, heart space and physical space.

- Clear your physical space of clutter and respect your surroundings.

- Know your worth and welcome financial prosperity into your life by tracking your income and outgoings.

- Clear your heart and mind with meditation and media cleanses, and let go of resentment.

- Be open to change, create a vision board, and make space in your life for opportunity and growth.

Part four:

The gift of giving

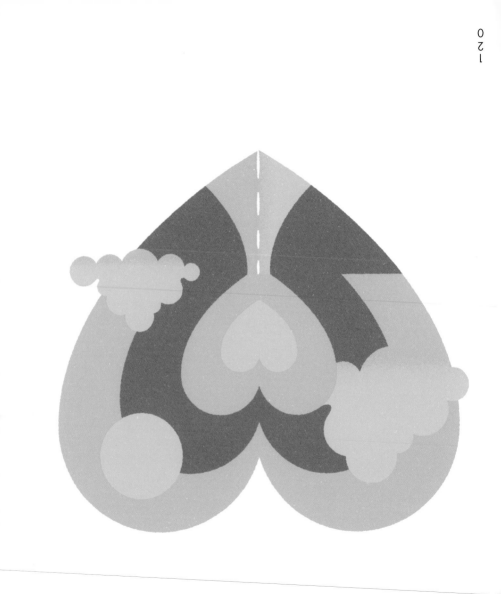

Be the gift that keeps on giving.

Giving for the simple act of giving is a blessing in and of itself. Give freely and abundantly. Giving is an opportunity to move out of lack, scarcity and selfishness. There are so many ways to give, from lending a helping hand to a friend in need to volunteering for a charity you believe in. Show up to parties with gifts in hand. Send flowers. Give on birthdays, holidays and any days. You can give anytime.

Give without a desired result.

Giving allows you to get used to sharing, and can help you get in touch with your own gifts and talents. So, get out of your shell. Start sharing your gifts.

Giving also allows another person the opportunity for receiving. It's a win-win. For many of us, receiving can be quite challenging. Remember, when someone is giving you a gift, just accept it. Allow the other person their own experience of giving.

It's all too easy to get wrapped up in our little and not-so-little problems. Sometimes, we forget there's a whole world, a whole solar system, a whole universe out there that moves on without us. Giving and being of service is a brilliant way to step outside of ourselves, to see a bigger purpose, to experience a world that's not all about you.

Giving is a heart-expander. Giving is a life-expander. Giving is a love-expander.

Create, give, expand – broaden your horizons.

Much of this book is about creating and receiving what you want. This chapter is about creating and *giving* what you want.

Give a gift away every day

Generally speaking, the idea for this practice is to set a timeline and go out of your way to give a gift away every single day.

The amount of money doesn't matter. You can do this even if you're flat broke. You can make gifts, but they have to be real, tangible gifts. Not 'I sent good thoughts and prayers to my friend today who is interviewing for a new job.' Find a flower, make a drawing on a cocktail napkin, or give your friend an all-expenses-paid luxury vacation to Fiji – the gift itself doesn't matter.

We did this with our Prosperity Family, and I received some beautiful, heartfelt stories. One that really struck me was about someone who had been struggling financially most of their life. They finally started to make a little bit more money, and one day they were shopping in a department store. Outside there was a woman with a list of items. She was a struggling single mother and this was around Christmas time. She was begging for money, or for someone to help her with these items. This person took the entire list and bought every single item, which came to a grand total of about £70 ($80).

When he came back and gave this woman everything, she started crying and said that nobody had ever helped her or taken care of her like that. Then he started crying too, and then I started crying as I read the post. It shows just how much is opened up by giving and gifting.

Conversely, my personal story was that always avoided certain situations so I couldn't be a giver. Having no money was keeping me very selfish. When I started this practice, I really had nothing. I mean, sometimes, I would literally just give a little stone. Sometimes it would just be something for a dollar, a fortune cookie that I had saved from a meal or a cute poem.

Pick an old friend who you haven't talked to in years and send them a gift. There are endless ways to give gifts. I sent somebody money via an app saying, 'Hey, go get your favourite matcha latte.' Get creative. It's about giving and sharing, and seeing what opens up for you.

I personally love this practice.

Community is immunity

Practice •

Surround yourself with people who are doing the things that you want to do.

Surround yourself with successful people.

One of my favourite teachings is: 'Recognise the other person is you.'

Success isn't only about money. When I was living in Los Angeles, I started to mix with people that were financially successful, but more importantly, they were doing things that were creative, artistic and visionary, from stylists to directors, film editors to sound engineers, published writers and painters to yoga teachers, shamans, singers and Grammy, Emmy and Oscar winners. Some of those people also led very spiritual lives. This really set the tone and made me realise, 'Hey, it actually is possible to do something creative and succeed.' This realisation was one of the greatest gifts that I have received in my life.

Not everyone was a multi-millionaire. Not everyone wanted to be. At the end of the day, they each proved that they could support themselves doing their creative endeavour, which, honestly, at that point, I couldn't even fathom.

When you surround yourself with people who are doing really well, or who do things well, you pick up that energy. It imprints something in your mind.

You may not always be able to physically surround yourself with great minds, but you do have the technology to access those people. Take note of their social media, follow their newsletters, take classes from experts, whatever the case may be. What you need is to see people create success.

I learned that it came down to doing what I love most, then monetising it. I was inspired by my friends. I had a tangible skill set. I got to make it into a thing, the same thing I'm doing now as I write this book. This book is an extension of that. There's a saying, 'Community is immunity.' Just make sure you are with and around people that elevate you, that inspire you, that want your growth; it's the best medicine.

It's really easy to get bitter when you're jealous of an old friend from high school who you still follow on social media, and who is having what appears to be the best life ever. They're married to the partner of their dreams, they have beautiful children, a yacht, or whatever the case is. If you find yourself going into a scarcity space, you need to look at their successes, the things you would like to have in your life, and celebrate them.

Say, 'Universe, thank you for showing me this, and thank you for showing me that this is absolutely possible. I, too, can do this.'

Celebrate.

Developing a community of people that really want each other to do well is one of the greatest gifts you can experience in this life.

For me, I've been very blessed to always have a strong support group. So many people believe in my work and vice versa. We support each other energetically and financially. If you're hanging out with a bunch of deadbeats and naysayers who aren't going anywhere, you start to become that too. It's a known fact that you start to become who you hang around with.

Look at the people, places and things that surround you. How do they influence you? Your subconscious is computing all of it.

Start finding communities that inspire you. Watch YouTube videos. Get involved. It's easier now than ever because there are so many groups online that also meet in person. If you still can't meet these people physically, there are so many other ways to connect. Use social media and the internet as a positive tools.

There are many specialities, talents, skills and interests in the world. It doesn't just have to be a job or a career. It can be anything you want to be good at. If you're interested in knitting, find people that are into knitting.

'Community is immunity' – yes, there are skill-set communities, but it's also good to have people in your life who are real, supportive and amazing, and who want you to do well. In turn, you have to want other people to do well, so celebrate their successes. Find people that are interested in the things you're interested in, and a lot will change; a lot will grow.

I'm beyond grateful for the extended community I have all over the world. I'm grateful for the very close friends that I have who are into what I'm into; we really encourage each other, whether it's in business, love or fun.

It makes life awesome. We need a lot more connection in our lives and we need to stay connected. We all know about isolation. This is not a book about that. This is a book about the opposite of that; so come together, get your crew, and, if you want to get really good at something, you need to be around people that are getting good at it too. No matter what it is – love, support, kindness, friendship – we need to celebrate each other.

Donate

Donating, also known as tithing,
is another great practice.

Donate money. Find causes that you believe
in, that resonate with your value and that
you'd like to help. Give money; you can give
your time too, but be sure to give financially.

The teaching is, when you make a donation,
you donate what you can afford plus just a
little bit more. You'll know the sweet spot when
it feels just ever so slightly uncomfortable.

Another of my favourite teachings says,
'Give to the unknown and it returns to you.'

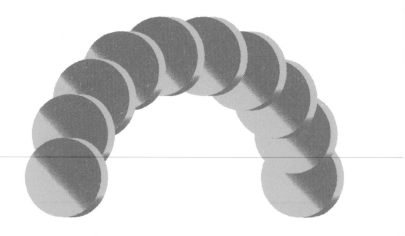

Random acts of service

The idea of this practice is to help somebody in need.

Surprise somebody you do or don't know and help them out. The first time I ever did this, I had a neighbour who struggled with walking. One day, as he was raking his leaves, I grabbed my rake and went out and started helping him. He didn't know what to say.

I think he felt strange at first that I was helping him, so I said, 'Don't worry about it.' I didn't want any money. 'You're my neighbour.' He was so appreciative because it was so physically difficult for him to do it. All I can say is that afterwards, I felt so elated and happy that to this day it is one of my favourite things I've ever done. I love this practice.

So, buy the guy in line behind you a cup of coffee. Help your neighbour move some furniture, pay for someone's lunch, volunteer at a local soup kitchen. There are endless ways to be of service.

Don't interfere. Just show up and help someone in need. That's all.

Create, don't compete

The universe is an abundant place.
There's plenty for everybody.

I mean, what more could be said? When you
are in competition, you're operating in a scarcity
mindset. You're focusing on having to beat somebody
else. You find yourself in a constant state of reaction,
meaning you can be thrown off your centre easily
because you're jealous or fearful of somebody
or another business or some rivalry. Just remember
all you have to do is focus on creating, on being
creative. Whatever it is that you're creating,
whatever type of content, whatever type of
product, whatever type of service or business,
focus on that, focus on your growth, and don't
worry about the rest. Remember, you were
created; the universe is a creative place.

Ultimately, there is no competition. One of the
fundamental teachings that I want this book to
impart is that there's only one you and you have
something very unique to share and give. Nobody
can compete with that. Why try to compete or
be something that you're not, why try to create
something that's not true? Let go of that.

It's an abundant universe; there's plenty
for everybody. Stay in that flow.

There's only one you, and you have something very unique to share and give. Nobody can compete with that.

Practise receiving

The ability to receive is very important. Consider the spiritual teaching: 'Make yourself a fit receptacle.' In order to receive these blessings and this prosperity, you need to create the space to receive it.

It's important to think outside of the box. Don't limit your definition of prosperity. The universe works in very mysterious ways, and there are many opportunities and an array of blessings. The universe is vast and endless and unexpected.

Allow the miracle. Don't overthink it. Say yes.

Practice •

Accept gifts. When someone wants to give you a gift, accept it. You are giving them the gift of allowing them to give.

Opulence practice

Practice •

Splurge on something nice for yourself.

Do this within reason, according to your financial means. The idea is to upgrade some items that you have, or maybe make a little splurge on something you've been thinking about, and spend a tad more than you would usually spend.

At one point in my life, I was looking into purchasing a luxury car. I was really nervous about it. My ego kept telling me I was being decadent and wasteful. I reached out to a friend of mine who I look up to. He's very successful in business and is also spiritually minded and grounded. I asked him what he thought, if I was just making an impulsive, crazy, lustful decision, and he said, 'Lean into it and buy the nice car, because you're in your car all the time. Every time you get into that car, you're going to love it. When you love it, that feeling just extends to everything else in your life.'

That was a huge lesson for me; it transformed materialism into the opulence of beautiful experiences. Every time I touched that steering wheel, every time I sat in that leather seat, every time I drove that car, which felt like driving a luxury couch, it elevated something in my consciousness beyond just having a nice car. The luxury experience in and of itself opened up a flow of success.

Palm practice

This is an interesting practice handed down to me that sets the tone for the day.

Practice •

Do this as soon as you wake up. Before you open your eyes, cover them with the palms of your hands. Slowly raise your hands and open your eyes, so that the first thing that you see is your palms.

The idea is that every morning you'll wake up and look straight at your destiny, which is said to be written on the palms of your hands.

In deeper esoteric teachings, it is the palm of the hand that receives blessings and abundance. I love this little practice, and the idea of waking up every day to welcome destiny into existence.

Create a sacred altar space

Practice •

Create a beautiful focal point for your prosperity and transformation. This can be a shelf, a table, a mantle piece, or maybe a special drawer that you keep private. How you do it is entirely up to you.

The idea is to have a beautiful space (according to your standards, beliefs and practices). A sacred space. A space you love. Put items there that are prosperous to you and that make you feel abundant. Crystals, flowers, inspiring pictures, spiritual trinket (tchotchkes), whatever you love.

An altar is a space that reminds you to have reverence. An altar is where we alter ourselves. It's like a 3D vision board. Use it for many of the practices in this book, such as your positive ___tions, as well as writing prompts, ___rds, whatever you like. Do you.

Morning sets the tone

Whatever you interact with when you first wake up will set the tone for the rest of the day.

If you have a really weird dream or a nightmare that gives you the creeps, you might feel mildly paranoid for the rest of the day. Starting with a healthy routine sets the day straight. When you start your day off right, it's infinitely easier to get through it.

Whatever practice you choose to employ, let it fit your lifestyle. Don't force it. Now that we have a kid, not much goes as planned per se, but life is happening for me, not to me, so waking up to his smile is an unanticipated blessing I take into whatever I do next.

Practice •

Think on this: what you do first sets the tone.

If you immediately wake up to a loud, annoying alarm, getting out of bed is a stressful situation. If you immediately check your phone, go straight to the news, check your emails, check social media – suddenly you're down a rabbit hole in a frantic attention war.

Try waking up to an alarm you love. If you wake up and set the tone you need to succeed, you will meet with more victories.

Clear the morning cobwebs

This practice is a great way to clear your head and get rid of your brain fog and any weird dreams that are still lingering from the long night before.

Practice •

Keep a notebook at your bedside. Upon waking, write three pages. Don't stop. Don't edit. Don't censor it. Don't think about it. Just let the writing happen. You're never going to read this again.

What you write doesn't matter. If you're thinking about it, you're doing it wrong. Write free-form; no thought. Three pages.

There's no regulation on the size of notebook. When I first started doing this practice, I had a rather large notebook, and it took me quite some time to fill three pages. So, I may have cut a few corners and got a smaller notebook, which really led to a lot of openings for me. Ultimately, though, it was all about clearing my head of all that mind clutter.

My wife did this practice for a year. She knows it was one of the things that led to a shift where she left her job to create her own successful business. Another friend did this for three months and swears it is what led to them getting off drugs, getting their head straight and going to art school.

Everybody's going to have a different story: this is a tried-and-true practice.

It's a big brain dump. Once I started doing it, it became something I couldn't stop doing every day, because it feels so right.

This is a great morning routine and a very important clearing practice.

- **Giving allows us to move out of scarcity and into prosperity.**

- **Give real, tangible gifts and donate money and time to causes you care about.**

- **Don't compete with others, but instead surround yourself with people who inspire you – and celebrate each other's successes.**

- **Receive with the same pleasure that you give.**

- **Adapt your morning practices and routines to begin your day with purpose and abundance.**

Crystals have vibrations that represent higher energies at work. Each crystal has an individual makeup of frequencies, signatures and patterns, which align with other energies. These work as a calling card or an antenna, if you will, to support your goals, so you can use them in addition to these other practices. They help set a tone and a pattern. Even if you don't believe in any of this, you could still take a crystal that you enjoy and use it as a focal point for creating intentions.

Now, I want to get into a few crystals that I've had great success working with.

The prosperity

of crystals

Citrine

This is the big one for me. Citrine is translucent orange and yellow. Some are very bright orange and others a little clearer with hints of yellow in them. Whatever the stone is, simply pick out one you love and that has a great vibe for you. Citrine is a money-maker. I was taught that the frequency pattern of citrine is very similar to the pattern that your brain experiences when you have actual cash currency. This means it helps attract money. You could go as deep as you want with this belief. Maybe that frequency is opening up channels in your brain, and those channels open channels to higher cosmic dimensions of consciousness that align you with attracting more prosperity. Ultimately, it's the law of attraction and intention towards prosperity. So you can go as far out as you like, or you could just say, 'This is kind of corny, but what the heck?' It's a beautiful stone so why not give it the benefit of the doubt.

Years ago, I did a trade with a phenomenal jeweller. She was so happy with my work, she gave me an incredibly beautiful citrine necklace, and taught me what citrine was used for. She knew I was trying to build up my financial reserve, and I was focused on making a lot more than I had been making, but I was still struggling.

She gifted me that necklace, and the very next day I got a slew of messages from prospective clients. This was right as I was beginning my business doing one-on-one sessions with people, and I was on the cusp of doubling my rate. I was so nervous, and such an 'under-earner' that I was terrified to go from charging £100 ($111) to £200 ($222). I had also been doing some heavy work with a life coach, who had encouraged me to double my rate, telling me that I was doing something great with my skill set in the city of Los Angeles, and with the type of clients that I had, I actually wasn't charging enough for my services.

As I sat there, wearing my citrine, reading messages from potential clients, a friend of another client of mine said she was hoping I had availability the following Tuesday at 12 p.m. or 2 p.m. Then she asked, 'Oh, by the way, how much do you charge?' I knew I was supposed to step up my rate to £200 ($222). I sat there for maybe 20 minutes paralysed with fear.

Well, there was something mystical sitting there in that necklace. I swear it helped line it all up. After hemming and hawing, I was about to message, 'My rate is £200 ($222), but if you can't afford that, we can work out a payment plan or whatever you can do...' but instead I squeamishly sent a straightforward message: 'My rate is £200 ($222).' Within a second, she replied, 'Great. I look forward to meeting you, I'll see you on Tuesday.'

That was one of the biggest consciousness openings I've ever had. It may seem crazy, but having the courage to charge my new rate was everything. Whether the power came from a crystal, a life coach or all of the above, I stepped up and I never looked back.

These things add up. I understand that on one level, it has nothing to do with that crystal. On another level, being cognisant of these intentions around the crystal and around money did help my personal transformation. When I started wearing citrine, I started getting more clients, and I started making more money. It's that simple.

All these practices work together to help you gain more prosperity. Citrine is one

piece of a greater puzzle. I know so many people that use it with great effect. Create a prosperity altar (see 'Create a sacred altar space' on page 135). Place citrine on the altar, along with other crystals and things that you love.

When my wife and I put an offer on our house, I left a little piece of citrine on the property with the intention of having our offer accepted. It was. Was it the piece of citrine that did it? It was one more tool that put positive energy around the situation. We came in swinging with a competitive offer, but so did many other people. It was our offer that was accepted. These little things add up.

I can honestly say that when I got that necklace and I charged my first client my new rate, my life absolutely shifted then and there. The few hundred dollars I made from seeing a few clients and odd side jobs grew into a few thousand dollars a week. It was significant, and it was life-changing. I attribute a lot of that to the citrine.

Practice •

Set more intentions, create more rituals, get focused. Crystals are a way to amplify intention. Let the universe know what you want; let your conscious and subconscious mind know what you want. Use citrine for prosperity and money.

Rose quartz

Another prosperous stone is rose quartz. It is the tried-and-true stone of love. It comes polished or raw, and in many shapes and sizes. Hold it in your hands. You may notice it's very calming and opening. The colour pink is very soothing as well. This is a great stone to hold intentions of love and for attracting a partner or improving the relationship(s) you have. It's simply sublime to feel more love in one's life. So why not try it?

Practice •

Get a piece of rose quartz and use it as a reminder to add more love to your life and also to remind you that you can attract love.

I put a beautiful piece in an altar space that was very sacred to me. My intention was love. My intention was to meet my partner. Before long, I met my soulmate, who is now the mother of my child.

Was it all because of a stone? Yes and no; it wasn't *just* because of a stone, but that stone reminded me to put positive intentions and positive energy towards what I wanted, which was a loving relationship, a wonderful soulmate relationship, a wife. It's a combination of all this work. I cherish the rose quartz. You can use it when you're feeling anxious or worried. It's just a nice reminder. Just go with it; don't overthink it. Allow it and let it be a reminder for love and that love is possible.

Lapis lazuli

Another favourite is lapis lazuli. This deep-blue stone with golden specks is called the Magician's Stone. You'll find it in the artwork of ancient Egypt. The idea is that the Magician's Stone holds a frequency of wisdom. In astrology, it is aligned with the planet Jupiter, which represents beneficence and wisdom. Jupiter carries the frequency of blessings and kindness. Lapis lazuli the stone of expansion. For me, expansion was having time to do the things that I love.

I utilise crystals, but I also utilise all these practices. I truly have a life that I love, and I have the time to love it and the money to do things I love with the people I love. I have a wonderful community of friends, and I don't have to work myself to the bone any more. I used to work from about 7 a.m. till about 11 p.m., just to make a couple of hundred dollars and I didn't have time for myself. All of that has changed and I don't have to work nearly that much. This has been a process. It didn't happen overnight, but it really built up.

There are many crystals and many other stones whose frequencies you can utilise. (Maybe that'll be another book at some point.) Keep an open mind. Set your own intentions. How much prosperity would you like to have? The truth is, we can all create abundant, fulfilling lives. YES, you too can have a life full of love, full of money, full of wisdom and plenty of time to participate in it.

Days of the week

Every day of the week has symbolic meaning. From astrology to mythology, there is a reason for their names and placement in the cycle of time. Whether you 'believe' in astrology or not, this is a great opportunity to use these prompts as an energetic grid. Think of it like a chess board and move your pieces strategically. Happy days.

Monday is the moon.

The day of inner self. This is great for inner work, subconscious work. The moon is nurturing. Take care of your family, do something that is inwardly creative and vibey.

Practices
- Resentments (page 112)
- I still love and accept myself (page 66)

Tuesday is Mars.

The day of war! This is the energy of right action. If you've been wanting to accomplish something or you're feeling like you need a breakthrough in your life, or you want to go to the gym, or do something physical. Tuesday is your day to go for it.

Practices

- Just say no (page 78)
- Change it up (page 110)

Wednesday is Mercury.

Mercury is our mind, communication and intelligence. Wednesday is the day for reading, studying, communicating and catching up on any type of writing. Just think of it like this: on a Wednesday, you're maybe just a little bit smarter than usual.

Practices

- Tracking numbers (page 92)
- Positive affirmations (page 63)
- Any practice that involves writing and accounting

Thursday is Jupiter.

Jupiter is the bestower of blessings, of kindness, of ease and abundance. Thursday is a great day to do some of this work. The energy of the universe is working in your favour. Let it.

Practices

- The 'yes' practice (page 76)
- Give a gift away (page 122)

Friday is Venus.

The day of love and art. It's romantic. It's a great day for a date. What can you upgrade? What can you make nicer? What can you make more beautiful in your life?

Practices

- Love list (page 35)
- Opulence practice (page 133)

Saturday is Saturn.

The taskmaster day. Saturn is discipline. It is work. It is effort. It is gumption. Saturday is a great day to do some home improvement, to practise any skill you want to get better at. Do anything that involves more disciplined effort. Saturday's a great day to do a little more.

Practices

- The accountability loose-ends list (page 104)
- Cold showers (page 37)

Sunday is the sun.

This is a very meditative energy. It is a day for reflection. A day to get centred. The sun carries strength and radiance, it also carries the reverent energy of prayer.

Practices

- Meditation (page 101)
- Create a sacred altar space (page 135)

If you're sensitive to it, you'll see how these energies flow naturally. Maybe you'll notice on Wednesday you get more phone calls, emails, messages, more people want to connect and communicate. Maybe you feel inspired to upgrade your look on Friday. Maybe the energy of Tuesday makes you a little more assertive. So, pay attention. If nothing else, use it as a loose outline.

Final
thoughts

In a world where it can feel like everything is stacked against us, my intention is to provide hope for possibility and transformation.

Transformation from hopelessness to hopefulness, from conflict to harmony, from confusion to clarity, from impossible to possible.

In this book, I have shared tools that when put into action can make a difference. Big and small. I personally know what's it like to be down and out, and I know what it's like to turn it all around. This is alchemy. I have turned despair into joy, I have turned fear into love, I have turned poverty into abundance. I have an amazing life, one I never thought was possible. I'm still growing, improving and expanding. I still have many changes I'd like to make for an even more abundant life. These are the tools I have used, and that others have also put into practice. I want to share the things that help me in the hope that they will help you, too. My dream is that if someone out there, even one person, utilises this book and it makes a difference in their life, then it is all worth it.

About the author

Remington Donovan is a master numerologist and mystic seer, trained in the spiritual wisdom of the ancients. He was quite literally born into the traditions of mysticism, spirituality and meditation, which naturally evolved into his now 30 years of experience practising with tarot and numerology. Along with performing thousands of private readings, Remington teaches and speaks all over the world. He hosts The Mystical Artists podcast and leads The Mystical Arts Mystery School. Remington takes great joy in the gift of seeing life's highest potential through numerology and in using that gift to guide and transform others. Remington lives in the enchanted Shires of Vermont with his wife, Jeana, and son, Isaiah Saint-Ra, where he unironically believes in the infinite possibilities of the universe.

Acknowledgements

I'd like to thank my cosmic wife and mother of our son, Jeana. You are the embodiment of abundance. Your love, guidance, support and belief in me and this work makes it all possible. Not to mention your attention to detail. I love you with all my heart and soul.

To my son Isaiah Saint-Ra, you are my little prosperity peanut. I love you beyond words. You have been the greatest gift I have ever received.

A deep and humble gratitude to all my teachers seen and unseen. It is your wisdom and guidance that wrote this book.

Special thanks to 'The Virgos', Vanessa and Mary Quinn, for keeping it organised and on point.

And to the wonderful team at Hardie Grant: Eve, Eila, Amelia and Bonnie. The universe conspired once again to create another gem. You really know how to make a beautiful book.

And to those still sick and suffering, don't give up. Miracles do happen.

Practices are in *italics*

n

o

p

Published in 2023 by Hardie Grant Books,
an imprint of Hardie Grant Publishing

Hardie Grant Books (London)
5th & 6th Floors
52–54 Southwark Street
London SE1 1UN

Hardie Grant Books (Melbourne)
Building 1, 658 Church Street
Richmond, Victoria 3121

hardiegrantbooks.com

British Library Cataloguing-in-Publication Data.
A catalogue record for this book is available
from the British Library.

Prosperity Practices
ISBN: 978-1-78488-610-3

10 9 8 7 6 5 4 3 2 1

Publishing Director: Kajal Mistry
Acting Publishing Director: Emma Hopkin
Commissioning Editor: Eve Marleau
Senior Editor: Eila Purvis
Design and Art Direction: A+B Studio
(Amelia Leuzzi + Bonnie Eichelberger)
Illustrations: A+B Studio (aandb.studio)
Copy-editor: Sophie Elletson
Proofreader: Tara O'Sullivan
Indexer: Cathy Heath
Production Controller: Gary Hayes

Colour reproduction by p2d
Printed and bound in China by Leo Paper Products Ltd.